MW00816945

Introduction to Bank Accounting

Jones Orumwense

Introduction to Bank Accounting

A Training Guide for Banking and Financial Institution

LAP LAMBERT Academic Publishing

Impressum/Imprint (nur für Deutschland/only for Germany)
Bibliografische Information der Deutschen Nationalbibliothek: Die Deutsche Nationalbibliothek verzeichnet diese Publikation in der Deutschen Nationalbibliografie; detaillierte bibliografische Daten sind im Internet über http://dnb.d-nb.de abrufbar.
Alle in diesem Buch genannten Marken und Produktnamen unterliegen warenzeichen-, marken- oder patentrechtlichem Schutz bzw. sind Warenzeichen oder eingetragene Warenzeichen der jeweiligen Inhaber. Die Wiedergabe von Marken, Produktnamen, Gebrauchsnamen, Handelsnamen, Warenbezeichnungen u.s.w. in diesem Werk berechtigt auch ohne besondere Kennzeichnung nicht zu der Annahme, dass solche Namen im Sinne der Warenzeichen- und Markenschutzgesetzgebung als frei zu betrachten wären und daher von jedermann benutzt werden dürften.

Coverbild: www.ingimage.com

Verlag: LAP LAMBERT Academic Publishing GmbH & Co. KG
Heinrich-Böcking-Str. 6-8, 66121 Saarbrücken, Deutschland
Telefon +49 681 3720-310, Telefax +49 681 3720-3109
Email: info@lap-publishing.com

Herstellung in Deutschland (siehe letzte Seite)
ISBN: 978-3-8484-8187-3

Imprint (only for USA, GB)
Bibliographic information published by the Deutsche Nationalbibliothek: The Deutsche Nationalbibliothek lists this publication in the Deutsche Nationalbibliografie; detailed bibliographic data are available in the Internet at http://dnb.d-nb.de.
Any brand names and product names mentioned in this book are subject to trademark, brand or patent protection and are trademarks or registered trademarks of their respective holders. The use of brand names, product names, common names, trade names, product descriptions etc. even without a particular marking in this works is in no way to be construed to mean that such names may be regarded as unrestricted in respect of trademark and brand protection legislation and could thus be used by anyone.

Cover image: www.ingimage.com

Publisher: LAP LAMBERT Academic Publishing GmbH & Co. KG
Heinrich-Böcking-Str. 6-8, 66121 Saarbrücken, Germany
Phone +49 681 3720-310, Fax +49 681 3720-3109
Email: info@lap-publishing.com

Printed in the U.S.A.
Printed in the U.K. by (see last page)
ISBN: 978-3-8484-8187-3

DEDICATION

To patience, my wife, Kenny, Winifred, Jeffrey, and Hillary, My Children.

PREFACE

"You have to know what something is before you know how to use it"

Introduction to Bank Accounting describes the most widely used accounting theory and practice with emphasis on what accounting is rather than on what it should be.

The bank, takes the view that banking is an exciting process and that accounting is the perfect window through which to see how economic events affect banking business. Because we believe that accounting aids the understanding of economic events and accounting builds on simple principles, this book introduces a number of concepts earlier than other textbooks. These early introductions are at the simplest level and are illustrated with carefully chosen examples from real organizations.

OUR PHILOSOPHY

Introduces the simplest concepts early, revisit concepts at more complex levels as the readers gain understanding and provide appropriate real-banking examples at every stage that's our philosophy.

We want readers to view accounting as a tool that enhances their understanding of economic events. Readers should be asking "After this transaction are we better or worse off". We believe that accounting provides a way to understanding what is happening and to answer that question you might think of the basic financial statements as scorecards in the most fundamental economic contests. Each year the financial statements help you answer the most important questions: Are you happy or sad? Did you make or loose money? Are you prospecting or just surviving? Will you have the cash you need for the next big step?

WHO SHOULD USE THIS BOOK?

The book presupposes no prior knowledge of accounting and is suitable for any undergraduate, or MBA students enrolled in a financial accounting course or Bankers who are already in the banking or financial institutions. It deals with important topics that all bankers and students should study. Our goals have been to choose relevant subjects matters and to present it clearly and accessibly.

This text is oriented to the user of financial statements but gives ample attention to the needs of potential accounting practitioners. The book stresses underlying concepts yet makes them concrete with numbers illustrations, many taken from recent corporate annual reports. Moreover accounting procedures such as transaction analysis, journalizing, and posting are given due consideration where appropriate.

Dr. Jones Orumwense

ACKNOWLEGEMENT

This book has been made possible through the direct and indirect corporation of various persons for whom I wish to express my appreciation and gratitude.

First and foremost, my intellectual debt is to those academicians and practitioners who have contributed significantly to the emerging field Accountancy and whose work has been quoted and used by me in writing this book. I am thankful to the following persons who have allowed me to reproduce their case studies in this book.

I am extremely grateful to Barrister Emmanuel Ajayi for helping in various ways despite his pre-occupation with his Doctoral research work. Dr. Kabir Haruna deserved my gratitude for his effort in preparing a section of the book particular thanks are also due to Dr. Yahaya Ibrahim who edited the manuscript of this book.

I am beholden to my family members for their blessings and encouragement. Patience, my wife, children Kenny, Winifred, Jeffrey and Hillary deserve special acknowledgement for willingly making me to work for realizing one of the major ambitions of my life. Patience, my wife also made a direct contribution by helping me to arrange the vast amount of information needed for the preparation of the manuscript.

I am indebted to my God for his effort he has put in for making this book a reality and giving it its present shape.

However, I accept the sole responsibility for any possible errors of omissions and commission and would be extremely grateful the readers of this book if they bring such mistakes to my notice.

I would further welcome any suggestion for making then ext edition of this book more useful to the readers.

Dr. Jones Orumwense

TABLE OF CONTENTS

A General Overview

Accounting is a service activity which measures quantitative information, usually financial in nature, and reports to various users for decision-making regarding an organization's economic activity.

The two approaches of accounting are cash-basis accounting and accrual accounting. With the cash basis of accounting revenues are recognized when cash is received, and expenses are recognized when cash is paid out. The primary advantages of cash-basis accounting are the increased reliability due to the fact that transactions are not recorded until complete and the simplicity due to the fact that fewer estimates and judgments are required. For most businesses the cash-basis of accounting for a period requires recognition and measurement of noncash resources and obligations. Cash-basis accounting is not in accordance with generally accepted accounting principles.

With the accrual basis of accounting revenues are recognized when sales are made or services are performed, and expenses are recognized as incurred. Revenues and expenses are recognized in the period in which they occur rather than when cash is received or paid out.

The following is an example of how misleading cash basis accounting can be. Assume that 1986 is the first year of operations for Gray Enterprises. In 1986, Gray had cash sales of $85,000 and cash expenses of $58,000. at December 31, 1986, Gray had accounts receivable from 1986 sales of $16,000 and accounts payable for 1986 expenses of $23,000. In 1987, cash sales were $160,000, and cash expenses were $172,000. Accounts receivable were $28,000, and accounts payable were at $18,000 at the end of 1987.

Cash-Basis

	1986	1987	Total
Revenue	$85,000	$160,000[1]	$245,000
Less: Expenses	58.000	172.000[2]	230.000
Earnings (loss)	$27,000	($12,000)	$ 15,000

[1]Includes $16,000 of 1986 credit sales.
[2]Includes $23,000 of 1986 expenses paid in 1987.

Accrual-Basis

	1986	1987	Total
Revenue	$101,000'	$172,000[2]	$273,000
Less: Expenses	81.000	167.000k	248.000
	$20,000	$5,000	$ 25,000

[1]$ 85,000 in cash sales + $16,000 in credit sales.
[2]$ 58,000 in cash expenses + $23,000 in credit expenses.
[3]$144,000 ($160,000— 16,000) in cash sales + $28,000 in credit sales.
[4]$l49,000 (172,000—23,000) in cash expenses + $18,000 in credit expenses.

The $10,000 difference in total earnings is due to the change in noncash resources and obligations over Gray Enterprises' two-year existence.

The two categories of accounting are financial accounting and managerial accounting. Managerial accounting provides special information for users within the organization. This information can be used in such decision-making processes as product costing and capital budgeting. It can also be used to measure a manager's performance in cost control and profit margins. Managerial accounting information must be useful and not cost more to gather than it is worth.

Financial accounting provides accounting information for use by those outside the organization. This information is used by investors and potential investors to determine the future benefits they will receive if they hold or acquire ownership in a business. Creditors and lenders use this information to assess the creditworthiness of an organization. This information is also used by employees, unions, customers, the general public, and governmental units.

Transactions, in accounting, are the result of the exchange of goods and/or services. Two factors allow the recording of a transaction—evidence and measurement. An exchange is an observable event and, therefore, provides evidence of business activity. This exchange takes place at a set price and, thus, provides an objective measure of the economic activity.

With the traditional accounting model a double-entry system of record keeping is used. The fundamental equation used with this system is

Assets = Liabilities + Owners' Equity

All transactions are analyzed and then recorded based upon their effect on assets, liabilities, and owners' equity. The increases and decreases in these accounts are recorded as debits or credits. In recording these transactions, the total amount of debits must equal the total amount of credits. The requirement that debits and credits must equal gives rise to the double-entry method of record keeping. In account form, the rules of debits and credits are as follows:

Debits	**Credits**
1. Increase assets	1. Decrease assets
2. Decrease liabilities	2. Increase liabilities
3. Decrease owners' equity	3. Increase owners' equity
4. Increase owners' drawing	4. Decrease owners' drawing
5. Decrease revenues	5. Increase revenues
6. Increase expenses	6. Decrease expenses

The accounting cycle records the effect of these economic transactions upon the assets, liabilities and owners' equity of an organization. The accounting cycle involves eight steps:

1. Analysis of Transactions

Each transaction must be analyzed before being recorded to determine the effect on the assets, liabilities, and owners' equity accounts. Asset, liability, and equity accounts are known as real accounts because they are not closed at the end of an accounting period. Revenue and expense accounts, however, are referred to as nominal accounts because at the end of an accounting period (usually a year), they are closed and their balances are reduced to zero. Therefore, the real accounts represent the financial position of an organization at any point in time. The nominal accounts represent the results of operations over a given period of time.

2. Journalizing of Transactions

After analysis to determine the affected accounts, transactions are recorded in the accounting journal, or journalized. Each account affected, the amount of the changes, and the direction of the changes (increases or decreases) are recorded. These transactions are recorded in the general journal or special journals, which serve a chronological record of all the economic transactions of an organization. Special journals group similar types of transactions to provide more efficient processing of data. These journals systemize the original recording of major recurring types of transactions such as cash receipts, cash disbursements, purchases, and sales. The general journal is used to make entries that do not fit in the special journals, to make adjusting entries at the end of the accounting period, and to make closing entries at the end of the accounting period.

3. Posting to the Ledger

The complete collection of all the accounts of an organization is the ledger. Transactions are posted to individual ledger accounts after being journalized. The ledger maintains the current balance of all the accounts.

Most organizations maintain subsidiary ledgers for accounts receivable and accounts payable, because it is difficult to determine amounts due from specific customers and amounts due to specific suppliers using the master Accounts Receivable account in the ledger. When using subsidiary ledgers, entries to the general ledger are totals for a specific period of time, e.g., weekly totals, from the special journals. The sums of all subsidiary ledgers should be equal to its master account in the general ledger.

4. Trial Balance and Working Papers

Working papers are large columnar sheets of paper for entering and summarizing the information necessary for making adjusting and closing entries and preparing financial statements. Working papers are prepared at the end of an accounting period and are for internal use only.

The first step in the preparation of working papers is the preparation of a trial balance. The trial balance lists all accounts with balances as of the end of the accounting period. Balances of the accounts are entered in the columns and totaled. If postings for the period are arithmetically correct, then debits will equal credits. The trial balance does not provide a means of determining whether transactions have been posted to the correct accounts or journalized and/or posted to the general journal.

5. Adjusting Entries

With the accrual system of accounting, certain adjustments must be made at the end of each accounting period. These adjusting entries convert the amounts actually in the accounts to the amounts that should be in the accounts for proper financial reporting. These adjusting entries allocate the cost of assets used in several accounting periods and revenues earned in several accounting periods, accrue revenues and expenses attributable to the current period that have not been recorded, and make appropriate end of period adjustments in the carrying value of certain assets, i.e., marketable securities and inventories.

With accrual accounting the cost of long-term assets must be apportioned to the periods which benefit from their use. The three types of long-term assets are productive assets such as buildings and machinery, wasting assets such a minerals, and intangible assets such as patents and copyrights. These assets are apportioned to periods through depreciation, depletion, and amortization. Another type of revenue and expense apportionment is to record the portion of unearned revenues earned during the year and the portion of a prepaid expense which expired during the year.

The following steps are necessary to make adjusting entries:
1. Determine the current balance in an account.
2. Determine the appropriate balance for the account.
3. Make the appropriate entry or entries to achieve the desired ending balances.

An adjusting entry may be necessary to reduce an asset to its market value. Some common adjustments are accounts receivable, inventories, and marketable securities. These accounts are adjusted by debiting an expense or loss account and crediting a contra-asset account.

6. Closing Entries
After posting adjusting entries, all nominal accounts with existing balances are closed to real accounts. These closing entries reduce the nominal account balances to zero to show the effect of these accounts on owners' equity and so that information for the next accounting period-may be accumulated. The following steps are required:

1. Close all revenue, gain, expense, and loss accounts to the Expense and Revenue Summary account. This account is used only at the end of an accounting period to summarize revenues and expenses for the period.

2. Close the Expense and Revenue Summary account to Retained Earnings.

3. Close the dividend account to Retained Earnings.

A post-closing trial balance is prepared after making all necessary closing entries. This provides a check against partial posting of closing entries. The post-closing trial balance reflects the balances to be included in the balance sheet at the end of the period.

7. Preparing Financial Statements

After preparing the adjusting entries and posting them to the work papers, an income Statement can be prepared using the income statement numbers from the workpapers.

After preparing the closing entries and posting them to the workpapcrs, the only accounts with balances should be the asset, liability, and owners' equity accounts. At this time, a Statement of Owners' Equity or Statement of Retained Earnings should be prepared. This statement summarizes the transactions affecting the owners' capital account balance or retained earning. Such a statement shows the beginning capital account, plus net income or less net loss, less owners' withdrawals or dividends. The ending capital account is then carried forward to the balance sheet, which helps to relate income statement information to balance sheet information.

Now it is time to prepare the Balance Sheet. The Balance Sheet is divided into assets, liabilities, and owners' equity and reflects the balances in these accounts at the end of the year.

8. Reversing Entries

Reversing entries, the final step in the accounting cycle, are recorded on the first day of the next accounting period. Reversing entries are prepared to reverse the effects of certain adjusting entries to which they relate. These entries reduce the possibility of including a revenue or expense at the time of the adjusting entry and including it again when the economic transaction occurs. The general rule on reversing entries is that all adjusting entries that increase assets or liabilities may be reversed. Therefore, the only adjusting entries that should be reversed are those which accrue revenues or expenses. Reversing entries are optional and are dependent upon an organization's bookkeeping system.

Financial statements issued for external users must conform to generally accepted accounting principles (GAAP). GAAP is established through general practice in the accounting field or by an authoritative body. The following are prominent authoritative bodies that help establish accounting principles:

1. Financial Accounting Standards Board (FASB)

The FASB has the primary responsibility of establishing accounting principles. The role of the FASB in the accounting procedure is to develop consistency in accounting principles, provide answers to emerging problems, and define the role of accounting.

The FASE issues two types of pronouncements: Statements of Financial Accounting Standards (SFASs or FASBs) which address specific accounting problems and Statements of Financial Accounting Concepts (SFACs) which provide an overview of accounting concepts and standards.

GAAP consists of the SFASs along with the Accounting Research Bulletins (ARBs) and Accounting Principles Board Opinions (APBs). The ARBs and APEs were issued by other authoritative bodies prior to the format of the FASB in 1971.

2. American Institute of Certified Public Accounts (AICPA)

The AICPA is the professional organization of certified public accountants and is composed primarily of CPAs in public practice. The AICPA is a major influence in the development of accounting standards and practices.

3. U.S. Securities and Exchange Commission (SEC)

The SEC is a regulatory agency created under the Securities and Exchange Act of 1934 to administer acts dealing with the interstate sale of securities. The SEC has the power to determine the accounting practices to be followed by companies under their jurisdiction and, therefore, ensure that investors have reliable information for use in investment decisions. The SEC works closely with the FASB to determine the issues that need to be addressed and to develop standards related to these issues.

4. American Accounting Association (AAA)

The AAA consists largely of accounting educators and its interest is, therefore, more theoretical. The AAA seeks to develop accounting theory, to improve education in accounting, and to encourage and sponsor accounting research. The AAA is not directly involved in establishing accounting rules, but they do influence the rules established.

Regulatory accounting principles and practices for banks generally follow GAAP. However, in four major areas regulatory accounting principles and practices differ from GAAP. They are as follows:

1. Goodwill

Goodwill is recognized as an asset under GAAP and amortized over its estimated useful life for a period not to exceed forty years. Banks cannot record goodwill but must expense it immediately. Bank regulatory authorities took the position that because the value and useful life of goodwill cannot be readily determined, no asset should be recorded. The Comptroller of the Currency recently relaxed this practice and allowed national banks to record goodwill and amortize it over its estimated useful life, not to exceed fifteen years.

Since the Federal Reserve Board requires that bank holding company financial statements conform to GAAP, bank holding companies can recognize goodwill as an asset and amortize it over its estimated useful life.

In late 1981 the Comptroller of the Currency recognized, in a tentative policy statement that a bank could record the acquisition of core deposits as an intangible asset. Core deposits are demand and savings deposits based on stable customer relationships. Therefore, the use of those funds is expected to continue for an extended period. An appraisal process involving analysis of the deposits acquired determines the value of a core deposit intangible, which is recorded as an asset On the bank's books.

2. Initial Stock Proceeds

Under GAAP, capital stock proceeds are split between the amount equal to the par value or stated value of the stock in the capital stock account and any excess proceeds are recorded in the additional paid-in capital account (surplus).

A bank is required to split its stock proceeds into three accounts. First, the paror stated value of the stock is recorded in the capital stock account. Second, an arbitrary amount, often equal to the capital account, is recorded as surplus. Thirdly, an amount, often equal to the expected initial operating losses of the new bank, is recorded as undivided profits (retained earnings). In the end, total stockholders' equity is the same as under GAAP.

In preparing bank financial statements, stock proceeds included in retained earnings can be dealt within one of two ways. The first method establishes a separate category within the stockholders' equity section that reflects the initial stock proceeds. The second method is to include a footnote that indicates the amount of initial stock proceeds included in retained earnings.

3. Cash-Basis Accounting

Under GAAP income is recorded as it is earned, and expenses are recorded when incurred (accrual method of accounting). Bank regulatory authorities allow banks with assets less than $5 million to report on the cash-basis.

4. Accounting for Hedging Transactions

GAAP is not clear on hedging transactions, but it appears that gains and losses on hedges of assets carried at cost should be deferred until the asset is sold and the transaction closed out. Gains and losses on hedges of assets carried at market should be marked to market.

Bank hedging transactions must be marked to market or carried at the lower of cost or market. If the asset is carried at cost, any gain or loss on the hedging transaction may be recorded in an entirely different period from the offsetting gain or loss on the asset hedged.

Modem accounting is based on historical cost data. Accounting transactions are recorded in terms of the actual dollars expended or received. Therefore, the income statement matches revenues from completed transactions with the historical costs incurred in producing these revenues. Income reported under the historical cost basis reflects increases in the net assets of an organization which result from transactions.

The primary objective of accounting is to provide users with financial data to assess the cash flow generating ability of an organization. The five general objectives of accounting are to:

1. Provide reliable information about changes in an organization's financial position, due to its income-producing efforts. This is the most important general objective due to the fact that this information indicates an organization's current and continuing ability to generate favorable cash flows.

2. Present earnings information in a manner that emphasizcs not only the sources of earnings but their trends. The inclusion of one past year's financial information for comparative purposes assists users in evaluating earnings potential.

3. Provide reliable financial information about economic resources and obligations of an organization. Resources represent potential cash inflows and obligations represent potential cash outflows. Sources of an organization's capital should be presented to aid in assessing an organization's ability to meet its short-term obligations and to indicate the resources available to exploit future opportunities.

4. Provide information about changes in net financial resources which result from financing and investing activities. This information is used in tinder- standing an organization's operations, evaluating its financial activities, and assessing its liquidity or solvency.

5. Disclose information relevant to statement users' needs in the footnotes to the financial statements. These additional disclosures should include the accounting procedures used in the statements, contingent obligations of the organization, any lease commitments, and any other disclosures deemed necessary in the professional judgment of accountants.

SFAC No. 3, "Elements of Financial Statements of Business Enterprises," dcl'ines the following ten accounting elements:

1. Assets — The probable future economic benefits obtained or controlled by a particular entity as a result of past transactions or events.

2. Liabilities— The probable future sacrifices of economic benefits arising from present obligations to transfer assets or provide services in the future as a result of past transactions.

3. Equity — The residual interest of the assets of an entity that remains after deducting its liabilities. In a business enterprise, the equity is the ownership interest.

4. Revenues — Inflows or other enhancements of assets or settlements of its liabilities (or a combination of both) during a period from delivering or producing

goods, render the services, or other activities that constitute the entity's ongoing major or central operations.

5. Expenses— Outflows or other using up of assets or incurrence's of liabilities (or a combination of both) during a period from delivering or producing goods, rendering services, or carrying out other activities that constitute the entity's ongoing major or central operations.

6. Gains — increases inequity (net assets) from peripheral or incidental transactions of an entity and from all other transactions and other events and circumstances affecting the entity during a period except those that result from revenues or investments by owners.

7. Losses — Decreases in equity (net assets) from peripheral or incidental transactions of an entity and from all other transactions and other events and circumstances affecting the entity during a period except those that result from expenses or distributions to owners.

8. Comprehensive Income — The change in equity (net assets) of an entity during a period from transactions and other events and circumstances from non owner sources. It includes all changes in equity during a period except those resulting from investments by owners and distributions to owners.

9. Investments by Owners in the Entity — Increases in net assets of a particular enterprise resulting from transfers to it from other entities of something valuable to obtain or increase ownership interest (or equity) in it. Assets are most commonly received as investments by owners, but that which is received may also include services or satisfaction or conversion of liabilities of the enterprise.

10. Distributions by the Entity to Owners — Decreases in net assets of a particular enterprise resulting from transferring assets, rendering services, or incurring liabilities by the enterprise to owners. Distributions to owners decrease ownership interest (equity) in an enterprise.

Revenues are produced by the sale of a product, performance of a service, or by allowing others to use the organization's resources for a fee.

The problem with recognizing revenue is determining when revenue is realized. The revenue recognition principle says that revenue should be earned and realized before it is recognized (recorded). Realization occurs when the increase in the value of net assets becomes available for the entity's use.

Generally, realization occurs at the time of sale of a product or performance of a service. Exceptions occur when material uncertainties exist about the collectability of certain receivables. In this case recognition is deferred until the uncertainties are removed.

Rents are fees earned from allowing others to use an organization's resources. These revenues are realized when use occurs and are treated like service revenues.

To determine income for an accounting period the accountant must match expenses of a period (cause) to the revenues realized from transactions completed during that accounting period (effects). The matching of revenues and expenses is based upon the assumed relationship between the production of revenue and the incurring of expenses. When a reasonable basis exists for associating costs with product units, these costs are recorded in an asset account and expensed when the product is sold. Costs that can't be associated with product units and are not expected to provide future benefits are treated as period costs and expenses in the current period. Executive salaries and office expenses are examples of period costs.

Summary

Accounting is a service activity which measures quantitative information and reports to various users for decision-making regarding an organization's economic activity.

The two basic approaches of accounting are cash-basis accounting and accrual accounting. Most organizations report on the accrual method, since the cash basis is not in accordance with GAAP.

Financial accounting and managerial accounting are the two categories of accounting. Managerial accounting provides financial information for users within the organization, and financial accounting information is used by those outside the organization.
Transactions which are the result of the exchange of goods and/or services are the basic component of accounting. Evidence and measurement are the two factors that allow the recording of a transaction.

The fundamental equation in the double-entry system of record keeping is:

Assets Liabilities + Owners' Equity

The increases and decreases in these accounts are translated into debits and credits for recording. The total debits must equal the total credits.

The accounting cycle involves eight steps: (1) analysis of transactions (2) journalizing of transactions (3) posting to the ledger (4) trial balance and working papers(S) adjusting entries (6) closing entries (7) preparing financial statements and (8) reversing entries.

Generally accepted accounting principles (GAAP) are established through general practice in the field or by an authoritative body. Financial statements issued for external use must conform to GAAP. The Financial Accounting Standards Board (FASB), the American Institute of Certified Public Accountants (AICPA), the U.S. Securities and Exchange Commission (SEC), and the American Accounting Association (AAA) are the primary authoritative bodies that help in the establishment of GAAP.

Typically regulatory accounting principles and practices for banks follow GAAP. The four major areas in which banking principles and practices differ from GAAP are: (1)

goodwill, (2) initial stock proceeds, (3) cash-basis accounting, and (4) accounting for hedging transactions.

Because modem accounting is based on historical cost data, accounting transactions are recorded based on the actual amount of dollars received or expended.

The main objective of accounting is to provide users with the financial information that will allow them to assess the ability of an organization to generate cash flow. The five general objectives are to (I) provide reliable information about changes in an organization's financial position, due to its income-producing efforts (2) present earnings information in a manner that emphasizes the sources and trends of earnings (3) provide reliable financial information about the economic resources and obligations of an organization (4) provide information about changes in net financial resources which result from the financing and investing activities of an organization and (5) disclose relevant information in the footnotes of the financial statements.

SFAC No. 3, issued by the FASB, defines the elements of the financial statements of an organization. SFAC No. 3 defines: equity, assets, liabilities, revenues, expenses, gains, losses, comprehensive income, investments by owners in the entity, and distributions by the entity to owners.

Revenues can be earned in three ways: (1) by the sale of a product (2) by the performance of a service or (3) by allowing others to use the organization's resources for a fee. The main problem with revenues is determining when revenue should be recognized. Based on the revenue recognition principle, revenue should be earned and realized before it is recognized and recorded.

Income for a period is based on the matching principle which matches expenses of a period (cause) to the revenues realized from transactions completed during that accounting period (effects). Expenses that can be associated with product units

16

(product costs) are recorded in an asset account and expensed when the product is sold. Period costs are costs that can't be associated with product costs and are not expected to provide future benefits. Period costs are expensed in the current period.

2

Balance Sheet

The balance sheet, sometimes called the Statement of Financial Position, provides information about an organization's assets, liabilities, and owners' equity at a specific point in time. The information on the balance sheet shows an organization's resources and obligations, which allows an outside party to evaluate its strengths and weaknesses. The assets represent the unexpired costs of past and current periods, the liabilities are obligations not yet discharged, and owners' equity is the owners' interest in the organization (assets minus liabilities). One way to look at the balance sheet is:

Earning Assets   Liabilities
+ Nonearning Assets   + Equity
Total Assets (footings)   Total Footings

In banking jargon, the terms earning assets and nonearning assets distinguish assets that earn interest from all other assets.

The balance sheet reflects these resources and obligations at historical cost, not at current valuation. This is related to the cost or exchange price principle. In an arms-length transaction (transaction between independent parties), the exchange price reflects both the historical cost and the value of the acquired asset or expense at the exchange date. These assets are carried at historical cost between the time of acquisition and disposal unless the asset loses value or utility through use. These depreciable or wasting assets are carried at their historical cost less an accumulated charge related to the decrease in their ability to provide future benefits.

17

The exchange price of an asset is dependent upon whether it is a monetary or nonmonetary asset. Determination of the exchange price of a monetary asset is relatively simple. It is fixed in money by contract or otherwise. In a nonmonetary exchange, the exchange price is based upon the fair market value of the asset surrendered. The fair market value of the asset received is used in those cases where the fair market value of the asset surrendered is not readily determinable.

When significant uncertainties exist related to assets and liabilities, the modifying convention of conservatism is applied. Any error in measurement should tend toward understatement rather than overstatement of net earnings and net assets.

Several criticisms have been leveled at the limitations of the balance sheet.
1. One criticism is that valuation is based upon historical cost and not current valuation. Because of this practice different organizations can have identical assets recorded at materially different amounts. If a user is concerned with the value of assets held (most creditors are), this practice limits the comparability and utility of the financial statements. Some critics have recommended that accounting information be adjusted for inflation or the use of supplemental disclosures based upon price level accounting or current value accounting.
2. Another criticism is the impact of accounting alternatives on balance sheet presentation. Different organizations may use different inventory costing methods or different methods of depreciation.
3. Another criticism is the absence of information about the liquidity and potential cash flows of an organization. A change in the preparation of financial statements to provide the information necessary to evaluate liquidity and potential cash flows may require major changes in the conceptual basis for preparing financial accounting reports.

Statements of Financial Accounting Concepts (SFAC) No. 3 defines assets as "probable future economic benefits obtained or controlled by a particular entity as a result of past transactions or events."2 The three essential characteristics of assets are:

1. There must be a probable future economic benefit.
2. The entity must be able to obtain the benefit or control the benefit.
3. The transaction or event giving rise to the entity's claim to, or control of, the benefit has already occurred.

SFAC No. 3 defines liabilities as "probable future sacrifices of economic benefits arising from present obligations of a particular entity to transfer assets or provide services to other entities in the future as a result of past transactions or events."3 The three essential characteristics of liabilities are:

1. There must be a probable future economic sacrifice.
2. It must be an obligation of the entity, not an obligation of the owners.
3. The transaction or event giving rise to the entity's obligation must have already occurred.

Equity as defined by SFAC No. 3 is "the residual interest in the assets of an entity that remains after deducting its liabilities." At any time prior to liquidation recorded owners' equity comes from three sources:

1. Capital contributed by nonowner sources that accrues to the owners.
2. Revenues and gains minus expenses and losses from past transactions.
3. Capital contributed by owners in past periods.

Accounts in the balance sheet are classified as to current and long-term assets, current and long-term liabilities, and owners' equity. A bank balance sheet is not classified as to current and long-term assets and liabilities, because, historically, bank assets and liabilities have not been easy to categorize in this manner.

Current assets are cash and other assets that will be converted into cash or used up by the organization within one year or within the operating cycle, whichever is longer. They are presented on the balance sheet in order or their liquidity.

Cash classified as current assets should be available to meet current obligations. Restricted cash is included only if the cash is restricted for current obligations, and then it should be disclosed. Cash can be combined with marketable securities, certificates of deposit, or time deposits. This practice is acceptable only if the marketable securities are commercial paper or U.S. Treasury notes.

Other types of current assets are marketable equity securities, accounts receivable, and inventory. Marketable equity securities, whether current or noncurrent, are shown at the lower of cost or market on the balance sheet. Accounts receivable are shown at face value less an allowance for doubtful accounts with appropriate disclosures. The presentation of inventories should include, by disclosure in the notes, the inventory cost flow assumptions used.

There are four main types of long-term assets:

1. Property, Plant, and Equipment   (no interest

Property, plant, and equipment should be shown with a deduction for depreciation. Disclosure of the depreciation methods used is required.

2. Noncurrent Investments

Long-term investments are generally shown at lower of cost or market.

3. Noncurrent Receivables

Where the interest rate reflected in the terms is fair and adequate compensation for the use of funds, long-term receivables are carried at face value. If the interest rate is not fair and adequate compensation then the receivable should be shown at the fair value of goods exchanged or the fair value of the receivable, whichever is more clearly determinable.

4. Intangible Assets (no\ nointerts)

Intangible assets are assets with no physical characteristics but derive their value from the advantages, privileges or rights they provide. Examples are patents, copyrights, trademarks, and goodwill. Costs of intangibles acquired in an arms-length transaction and specifically identifiable are capitalized and amortized in future periods.

Bank balance sheets normally have the following asset accounts:

1. Cash and Due from Banks

Cash and due from banks reflects the total of all coins and currency on hand, all funds held in deposit accounts with other commercial banks which are in the process of collection, and for member banks, the required reserve balance kept with the Federal Reserve Bank. Any material interest-bearing deposits with correspondent banks should be disclosed separately.   not int beaing

2. Investments

The investments account reflects securities purchased and held for a bank's own portfolio. This practice allows a bank to maintain liquidity while maximizing earnings on sometimes-idle funds.

The allowable types of securities are normally stipulated by law and bank supervisory agencies. Investment securities are classified in the balance sheet as U.S. Treasury securities; obligations of federal government agencies; obligations of states, municipalities and their political subdivisions; and other securities.

Marketable equity securities are carried at the lower of aggregate cost or aggregate market value at the balance sheet date. A valuation allowance is used to account for the excess of aggregate cost over aggregate market value.

Accumulated changes in this valuation allowance should be reflected separately in the equity section of the balance sheet. The related provisions should be debited to income and classified in the income statement with securities gains and losses. If the loss is temporary, the allowance is reduced or eliminated as conditions change.

3. Loans

Generally loans are the largest asset of a bank. Loans include all obligations to the bank, whether secured or unsecured, and unauthorized loans, such as overdrafts on demand deposit checking accounts. A bank's lending activities are normally classified as commercial loans, installment loans, real estate mortgage loans, and lease financing.

Loans are reflected as an aggregate amount with a deduction for any unearned discount, the allowance for possible loan losses, and any unauthorized loan origination fees. Any related accrued interest receivable is included in other assets or stated separately. Any material unamortized loan fees should be presented as other liabilities. Lease financing is classified as loans and valued by adding the aggregate lease payments receivable plus estimated residual value, less the unearned income and allowance for losses.

4. Fixed Assets

A typical bank's fixed assets include land occupied by the bank or held for future expansion, bank buildings and improvements, leasehold improvements, furniture, fixtures, and equipment.

Fixed assets are normally presented in the balance sheet net of accumulated depreciation and amortization. The basis of valuation should be disclosed in the notes. Property, such as repossessed collateral, should be reflected in other assets.

Current liabilities are obligations, usually due within one year which are expected to require the use of resources properly classified as current assets or to create other current liabilities. Some typical current liabilities are accounts payable, accrued salaries payable, dividends payable, warranties, and the current portion of long-term debt (due within one year).

The liability accounts of a bank are the several types of deposits that provide funds for a bank. The major liability of a bank is demand (checking) and time (savings) accounts used by customers to draw on or have as savings. Another liability of a bank is borrowed funds. These funds are borrowings from the Federal Reserve Bank or the Federal Home Loan Bank Board or through issuing debentures, capital notes, commercial paper, and mortgage notes.

The other liabilities account consists of expenses that have been accrued but not yet paid, such as payroll, income taxes, accounts payable, etc.

Deposits are normally presented as: demand deposits, time deposits, and certificates of deposits of $100, 000 or more. Any material negotiable order of withdrawal (NOW) accounts should be disclosed separately.

Borrowings from the Federal Reserve banks are grouped with promissory notes and reported like other borrowed funds. Mortgages payable are reported separately. Long-term debt, such as debentures and capital notes, are grouped together as Notes Payable.

Long-term liabilities are those liabilities not classified as current. These include bonds and notes payable and certain lease obligations not due within the next year or accounting cycle.

The business form of an organization determines the owners' equity sections of its balance sheet. Capital accounts are used with a sole proprietorship or partnership. Corporate entities reflect contributed capital, undistributed earnings, and unrealized increments or decrements to stockholders' equity.

Contributed capital consists of the legal capital based upon the par or stated value of an stated value. For stock with no par or stated value, contributed capital is the actual amount received for the stock.

The amount of dividends distributed is generally at the discretion of the board of directors, unless restrictions are imposed by debt agreements, treasury stocitheld, or other corporate activities. Retained earnings generally establishes the maximum amount of assets which may lie distributed.

Balance sheets rarely present any unrealized increments to stockholders' equity. These rare cases are items such as the discovery value of mineral deposits and oil and gas reserves. When the market value of the noncurrent portfolio of marketable equii securities is lower than the cost than an unrealized decrement to stockholders' equity is presented.

A bank's equity section normally presents paid-in-capital and retained earnings sometimes referred to as undivided profits. Capital stock and the surplus account make up the paid-in-capital. The capital stock account reflects the total parorstated value of both preferred and common stock which is authorized, issued, and outstanding at the balance sheet date. The surplus account represents the portion of paid-in-capital in excess of the par or stated value of the capital stock.

The retained earnings account represents the accumulated revenues and expenses of a bank. Dividends are generally paid firm this account.

APB Opinion No. 22. "Disclosure of Accounting Policies," states the following:
"Disclosure should encompass those accounting principles and methods that involve any of the following:

A selection from existing acceptable alternatives.

Principles and methods peculiar to the industry in which the reporting entity operates, even if such principles and methods are predominantly followed in that industry.

Unusual or innovative applications of generally accepted accounting principles."

Other important disclosures are any information that elaborates on balance sheet items. One method of disclosure is parenthetical explanations in the body of the financial statements. Users are more likely to' notice parenthetical explanations; therefore, they are more likely to be used in decision-making. Where a lengthy explanation is required, it should be in a footnote at the bottom of the page or explained in a series of notes to the financial statements.

Supporting schedules are often used awd5sclosures to provide additional information about the composition of certain assets or liabilities.

Contingencies must be disclosed so as not to mislead any users of the financial statements. Contingences are existing conditions which, when resolved through the occurrence or failure to occur of an event, may result in a gain or loss.

Subsequent events are events or transactions which occur between the balance sheet date and the date of the external auditor's report on the financial statements and which have a material effect on the financial statements. Omission of these events would make the financial statements misleading.

One type of subsequent event includes events that provide additional evidence about conditions that existed at the balance sheet date. This type of event must be incorporated into the balance sheet through adjustments.

The second type of subsequent event arises between the balance sheet date and the auditor's report date but does not provide additional information about a condition existing at the balance sheet date. This does not require adjustment of the financial statements. Most of these subsequent events are included in the notes to the financial statements. If significant, the historical financial statements should be accompanied by pro-forma financial statements which should the effect of the event as if it had occurred prior to the balance sheet date.

Summary

The balance sheet provides financial information about an organization's assets, liabilities, and owners' equity at a specific point in time. These accounts are reflected on the balance sheet at historical cost, not at current valuation. Historical east is related to the cost or exchange price principle. The exchange price of a monetary asset is fixed in amount, while the exchange price of a nonmonetary asset is based upon the fair market value of the asset surrendered. In cases where the fair market value of the asset surrendered is not readily determinable, the fair market value of the asset received is used.

The limitations of the balance sheet have drawn criticisms. One criticism relates to the use of historical cost date which limits the comparability and utility of the financial statements. Another criticism is the impact of accounting alternatives on balance sheet presentation. A final criticism is the absence of the information about the liquidity and potential cash flows of an organization.

SFAC No. 3 defines an asset. The three essential characteristics of an asset are (1) there must be a probable future economic benefit (2) the entity must be able to obtain or control the benefit and (3) the transaction or event giving rise to the organization's claim to, or control of, the benefit has already occurred.

SFAC No. 3 also defines liabilities whose three essential characteristics ate (1) there must be a probable future economic sacrifice (2) it must be an obligation of the organization and (3) the transaction or event giving rise to the entity's obligation must have already occurred.

SPAC defines equity as "the residual interest in the assets of an entity that remains after deducting its liabilities." The three sources of owners' equity arc (I) capital contributed by nonowners that accrues to the owners (2) revenues and gains minus expenses and losses from past transactions and (3) capital contributed by owners in past periods.

The balance sheet is divided into current and long-term assets, current and longterm liabilities, and owners' equity. Bank assets and liabilities are not divided into current and long-term.

Current assets are cash and other assets that will be converted into cash or used up by the organization within one year or the operating cycle whichever is longer. All other assets are classified as long-term. The typical asset accounts of a bank's balance sheet are cash and due from banks, investments, loans, and fixed assets.

Current liabilities are typically obligations due in one year or the operating cycle, whichever is longer. Current liabilities are expected to require the use of current assets or to create other current liabilities. All other liabilities are long-term. The liabilities of a bank are the several types of deposits that provide finds for a bank.

The owners' equity section of a balance sheet is determined by the business form of an organization. Sole proprietorships and partnerships use capital accounts, while corporations reflect contributed capital, undistributed earnings, and unrealized increments or decrements to stockholders' equity. The owners' equity section of a bank's balance sheet normally presents paid-in capital and retained earnings.

APB Opinion No. 22 requires disclosure if an accounting principle or method involves (1) a selection from existing acceptable alternatives 2) principles and methods peculiar to an organization's industry or (3) unusual or innovative applications of GAAP.

Disclosures can be made in the form of a parenthetical explanation in the body of the financial statements, supporting schedules, or footnotes.

Contingencies and subsequent events must be disclosed. Subsequent events are events or transactions which occur between the balance sheet date and the auditor's report date and which have a material effect on the financial statements. One type of subsequent event provides additional evidence about conditions that existed at balance sheet date, while the second type does not. The second type is a new event or transaction.

3

Income Statement

The income statement or Statement of Earnings reports the profitability of an organization for a stated period of time. Most preparers and users of financial information consider this the most important of the basic financial statements since it measures the success of an organization.

One of the primary objectives in financial reporting is to provide an income statement which emphasizes the earning power of an organization. Earning power is the normal level of earnings expected to be attained or maintained in the future. To determine the normal level, a distinction should be made between revenues realized from profit-directed activities and revenues realized from unusual or nonrecurring sources.

Another primary objective in financial reporting is to provide information about the quality of earnings. One factor in evaluating the quality of earnings is the source, since earnings from continuing activities are more likely to be sustainable than earnings from unusual or nonrecurring sources. Distinctions in quality should also be made for the sources of earnings from continuing activities, since these earnings may have different levels of uncertainty and thus be of variable quality.

Two approaches to income measurement are used. One approach is the capital maintenance approach (asset and liability view) which takes the net assets or capital values based on some valuation and measures income by the difference in capital values at two points in time. The transactions approach (revenue and expense view) focuses on the activities that occur during a given period and presents the components that comprise the change. Each transaction is analyzed and summarized in the income statement.

The major difference in the approaches is the point at which revenues are deemed to be realized and costs incurred or the point at which changes in the value of assets should be recognized. The basis of the asset and liability view is the accretion approach which recognizes changes in value throughout the production, sale, and collection cycle as earnings. The problem with this approach is measuring the changes in asset values before all material uncertainties have been eliminated. The basis of the revenue and expense view is the transactions approach which realizes the increase in the value of assets at the point of the most significant economic event in the production, sale, and collection cycle. The most significant economic event is generally economic transactions.

Realization is a concept used in determining when to recognize or record revenue. As discussed before, revenue can be earned by (I) performing a service, (2) selling a product, or (3) renting an organization's resources to others. For these activities revenue is realized as services are performed, at the point of sale of a product, or as rent is earned. To accrue earnings from performing services or renting resources to others generally requires adjusting entries, since the revenues are generally earned in one period and collected in a later period.

Revenue maybe recognized during the production process if the following four conditions are met:
1. No material uncertainties exist about the selling price of the product
2. No material uncertainties exist with respect to future costs to be incurred.
3. Units of the product are interchangeable.
4. Collection of the proceeds from future sales is reasonably assured.

The percentage-of-completion method for recognizing revenues and expenses on long-term construction contracts is one common case of revenue recognition during the production process. Delaying recognition of these revenues would result in understatement of earnings in the early periods of the contract and overstatement in the period of completion.

Material uncertainties with respect to future costs is generally no longer relevant at the completion of production. The important criteria for recognizing revenue at this time are the interchangeability of units, removal of material uncertainties as to the selling price, and assurance of the collection of sale proceeds. Some products generally considered for revenue recognition between the completion of production and the point of sale am precious metals and oil and gas reserves.

With installment sales, sales of franchises, and sales of real estate. revenue may not be recognized until after the point of sale. Recognition after the point of sale is justified if material expenses remain to be incurred and these expenses cannot be reasonably estimated or if the assets received in the exchange transaction cannot be valued with reasonable accuracy.

Expenses recognized in an accounting period should include product and period costs. Product costs are costs matched with products sold or services rendered during the period. Period costs are costs associated with the current period and require immediate recognition. Immediate recognition is appropriate when costs provide no discernible future benefits or attempts to establish the existence of future benefits and the period in which these benefits expire serve no useful purpose.

ARE Opinion No. 9, "Reporting the Results of Operations," recognizes the need to isolate earnings from normal, recurring operations of the period and the need to show the results of all the profit-directed activities of the period. This approach includes earnings from normal, recurring items and earnings from extraordinary items with clear distinctions made in the reporting of the items.

The two types of statement formats are the single-step income statements and the multiple-step income statements. Banks sometimes refer to the multiple-step format as the "interest margin" type format.

With the single-step format two groups exist, revenues and expenses. Expenses are deducted from revenues to arrive at net income or loss for the period. The advantage of this format is its simplicity of presentation and the elimination of potential classification problems due to the absence of any implication of the priority of one type of expense over another.

With the multiple-step format both revenues and expenses are divided between operating and non operating activities. Then expenses are classified and grouped according to functions. This provides more information to the user of the financial statements, such as:
1. Information about margins, relative sales, and cost of goods sold.

2. Better evaluation of the performance Of management and future prospects of an organization due to the separation of revenues and expenses from product sales, services, and investment.
3. Better evaluation of growth potential and performance of an organization due to the functional classification of revenues and expenses between merchandising and manufacturing.

The income statement is divided as follows:
1. Operating Section. Reports the revenues and expenses of an organization's principal operations.
    a. Sales or Revenue Section. Reports the pertinent facts about sales, discounts, allowances, returns, and other related information and arrives at the net amount of sales revenue.
    b. Cost of Goods Sold Section. Reports the cost of goods sold to produce sales and adequately details the components of this cost.
    c. Selling Expenses. Reports expenses incurred from the organization's efforts to make sales.
    d. Administrative or General Expenses. Reports expenses of the general administration of the organization's operations.
2. Non operating Section. Reports revenues and expenses resulting from secondary or auxiliary activities of the organization.
    a. Other Income. List of incomes earned from non operating transactions, generally shown net of related expenses.
    b. Other Expenses. List of expenses or losses incurred from non operating transactions, generally shown net of related incomes.
3. Income Taxes. Reports as a separate item the amount of federal and state income taxes.
4. Discontinued Operations. Reports material gains or losses on the sale of a segment of the organization.

5. Extraordinary Items. Reports material amounts of unusual and infrequent gains and losses.
6.

6. Earnings Per Share.

In the past bank income statements traditionally presented a two-tiered disclosure showing both income before securities gains and losses and net income. Securities gains and losses were often spoken of as being "below the line" and other income and expense items as being "above the line."

Banks and bank holding companies are now required to report gross securities gains or losses as a part of other income. This change was instituted with years ending on or after December 31, 1983. The SEC first adopted this change for publicly held bank holding companies, and it was later adopted by the AICPA, whose statement of position states:

"Net investment securities gains or losses should be presented in a separate line, on apretax basis, in the other income' section of a bank's income statement. If not material, they may be included in 'other income'."

'Prior periods' interim and annual financial statements should be restated to conform with the one-step format.

Another aspect of financial reporting that differs between banks and other types of organizations is the allowance for possible loan losses or reserve for bad debts. For income tax purposes, banks can deduct a provision for loan losses based on an arbitrary formula instead of actual experience. This has, at times, resulted in an allowance significantly greater than necessary. Since bankers viewed the provision was charged to retained earnings. Tn 1968 the ATCPA published the Bank Audi: Guide, which required the provision for loan losses to be charged against income. The amount not expensed (excess of amount required for managerial and financial reporting purposes) is recorded as a reserve for contingencies and presented as a component of stockholders equity. The difference in the provision as shown on the income statement and the federal income tax return is shown as deferred taxes on the balance sheet. Since estimates involve uncertainties, changes in accounting estimates will occur.

Estimates that may change are:
1. Estimated lives of fixed assets.
2. Percentage of accounts receivable or sales which will prove to be uncollectible.
3. Costs of construction on long-term projects.

These changes are reported in the period of change and any future periods that may be affected. The two main reasons for not accounting for changes in estimates as prior period adjustments are:
4. These changes tend to be immaterial. This practice might erode public confidence in the accounting profession and the information in the financial statements.
5. Any portion of the effect assigned to past periods would never be reflected in an income statement. An organization could overstate earnings in certain periods by underestimating certain costs.

Another type of accounting change is a change in accounting principle. Some examples of a change in accounting principle are:
6. A switch from one inventory costing method to another.
7. A change in one depreciation method to another.
8. A change to or from full costing for oil and gas reserves.
9. A change in the method of accounting for a long-term construction contract.

These changes are reported by including the cumulative effect of the change in earnings in the period of the change. Some special cases require adjustment of the beginning retained earnings and a retroactive adjustment of statements of prior periods which are presented for comparative purposes. The cumulative effect of this change is disclosed as a separate item, net of tax, following extraordinary items in the income statement

A special type of accounting change is a change in the reporting entity. This change results in a different group of companies comprising the reporting entity. These changes are limited to the following three basic situations:
1. Changing the companies included in combined financial statements.
2. Changing specific subsidiaries comprising the group of companies for which consolidated financial statements are presented. This does not include changes in the group of companies due to the purchase or sale of a subsidiary.
3. Presenting consolidated or combined statements in place of statements of individual companies.

This change requires restatement of all financial statements presented so as to maintain comparability. Disclosures required for this type of change include the reasons for the change, the nature of the change in the reporting entity, and the effect of the change on earnings before extraordinary items, net earnings, and the related per share amounts. Disclosure in future years is not required.

There are only two types of prior period adjustments:
1. Correction of an error in the financial statements of a prior period.
2. Adjustments resulting from pre-acquisition operating loss carry forwards of purchased subsidiaries.

These prior period adjustments are charged or credited to beginning retained earnings and are not included in the determination o income for the current period. For comparative purposes any prior period financial statements presented should include any adjustments in the income statement to reflect retroactive application.

Extraordinary items are not treated as revenues or expenses from operations. To qualify as extraordinary, an event or transaction must meet both of the following criteria:

1. Unusual in nature - The event or transaction should possess a high degree of abnormality and be of a type unrelated to the ordinary and normal activities of an entity, taking into account the environment in which the entity operates.

2. Infrequent in occurrence - The event or transaction should be of a type that would not reasonably be expected to recur in the foreseeable future, taking into account the environment in which the entity operates.

APB Opinion No. 30, "Reporting the Results of Operations," states: "The environment of an entity includes such factors as the characteristics of the industry or industries in which it operates, the geographic location of its operations, and the nature and extent of governmental regulation."

APB Opinion No. 3 specifies the following items should jj be treated as extraordinary:
1. Gains or losses on disposal of a segment of a business.
2. Adjustments of accruals on long-term contracts.
3. Write-downs or write-offs of receivables, inventories, equipment leased to others, deferred research and development costs, or other intangible assets.
4. Gains or losses from sale or abandonment of property, plant, or equipment used in the business.
5. Effects of a strike, including those against competitors and major suppliers.
6. Gains or losses from exchange or translation of foreign currencies, including those related to major devaluations and revaluations.

In the income statement extraordinary items are presented in a separate section net of tax. Extraordinary items are presented after gain or loss on discontinued operations and before cumulative effect of a change in accounting principle.

Discontinued operations, which refers to those of a separate line of business or class of customers, is reported as a separate line item in the income statement. The amount of the gain or loss on disposal of a segment of a business is determined by the results of operations of the disposed segment, net of applicable income taxes, and any gain or loss on the disposal, net of applicable income taxes.

The effects of discontinued operations are presented in the income statement after income from continuing operations and extraordinary items.
Items that do j qualify as disposals of segment of a business are:
1. Disposal of part of a line of business.
2. Shifting of production or marketing activities for a particular line of business from one location to another,
3. Phasing out of a product line or class of service.
4. Other changes occasioned by a technological improvement.

Earnings per sham (EPS) is calculated by dividing the earnings available to common stockholders by the weighted average number of shares outstanding. EPS must be computed for both earnings before extraordinary items and earnings after extraordinary items and prominently reported on the income statement. This information can be used to assess the past performance and future prospects of an organization and in choosing between alternative investments.

One of the objectives of accounting is to disclose information related to the financial statements that is relevant- to statement user needs. Items such as the accounting policies of an organization and any contingent liabilities of an organization should be disclosed. The necessary disclosures of an organization are a function of the activities of the organization.

Summary

The income statement or Statement of Earnings provides financial information on the profitability of an organization for a stated period of time. A primary objective of the income statement is to emphasize the earning power, or normal level of earnings expected to be maintained by the organization. Another objective of the income statement is to provide information on the quality of revenues by defining the source of revenues, indicating the reliability or uncertainty of these funds.

The two approaches to income measurement are the capital maintenance approach and the transactions approach. The difference in the two approaches is the point of revenue realization and cost incurrence or the point at which changes in the value of assets should be recognized. The capital maintenance approach (asset and liability view) recognizes changes in asset values throughout the production, sale and collection cycle. The transactions approach (revenue and expense view) recognizes the accretion of asset value at the point of the most significant economic event in the cycle, which is generally and economic transaction.

Revenue is recognized in financial reporting when services am performed, at the point of sale of a product, or as rent is earned. Revenue may be recognized during the production process only if certain conditions are met. Revenues from long-term construction contracts are commonly recognized on the percentage-of-completion method. Delaying recognition would misstate revenues in subsequent periods.

If material expenses remain to be incurred and these expenses cannot be reasonably estimated, or if the asset received in the exchange transaction cannot be valued with reasonable accuracy, then recognition of revenues for the point of sale is justified.

Product costs are expenses matched with products sold or services rendered during the period. Other costs and period costs, and deserve immediate recognition when they provide no future benefits.

APB No. 9 requires that earnings from recurring transactions be distinguished from extraordinary earnings.

The two types of income statement formats are the single-step income statement and the multiple-step income statement. The single-step fomiat groups all revenues together and all expenses together. Expenses arc deducted from revenues to arrive at net income or loss for the period. Multiple-step income statements generally follow the following format:

Operating Section

Sales and Revenues	xxx
Cost of Goods Sold	(xxx)
Gross Profit	xxx
Selling Expenses	(xxx)
General and Administrative Expenses	(xxx)
Income from Operations	xxx

Non operating Section

Other Income	xxx
Other Expenses	(xxx)
Income Taxes	(xxx)
Results of Discontinued Operations	xxx
Extraordinary Items	xxx
Net Income	xxx
Earnings Per Share	xxx

Certain aspects of financial reporting differ between banks and other types of organizations. Banks and bank holding companies are required to report gross securities gains or losses as a part of other income. Treatment of provisions for loan losses differs for financial reporting purposes and tax purposes.

Changes in accounting estimates are reported in the period of change and future periods. Changes in accounting principles arc reported by including the cumulative effect of the change in earnings in the period of change. Special cases require adjustment of beginning retained earnings and retroactive adjustment of statements of prior periods presented for comparison. Changes in reporting entity require restatement of all financial statements and disclosure of the reasons, nature and effects of the change.

Prior period adjustments are made only to correct an error in prior period statements or to make adjustments resulting from pre-acquisition operating loss carry forwards of purchased subsidiaries. Prior period adjustments are charged or credited to beginning retained earnings.

Items unusual in nature and infrequent in occurrence are extraordinary items. Extraordinary items are presented in a separate section of the income statement net of tax.

The gain or loss on disposal of a segment of a business is determined by the results of operations of the disposed segment, net of applicable income taxes, and any gain or loss on the disposal, net of applicable income taxes. This gain or loss is presented on the income statement after income from continuing operations and extraordinary items. Earnings per share must be computed to assess the past performance and future prospects of an organization. Other relevant issues such as accounting policies and contingent liabilities should be disclosed in the footnotes.

4

Statement of Retained Earnings

And Statement of Changes in

Financial Position

A statement of retained earnings provides a reconciliation of the beginning balance of retained earnings to the year-end balance. This statement reflects the transactions affecting shareholders' equity, including the net earnings or loss from the income statement. In recent years there has been a trend toward presenting a statement of shareholders' equity rather than a statement of retained earnings.

The statement of shareholders' equity presents the beginning and ending balances of retained earnings, net income or loss for the period, changes resulting from prior period adjustments, dividend distributions, and changes resulting from capital transactions. Changes resulting from capital transactions include the sale of capital stock, issuance of capita] stock as part of a stock option plan, and purchase of treasury stock.

The statement of changes in financial position provides information on all resources provided during a period and the uses of these resources (financing and investing activities) for an organization. Financial statement users can then see what caused changes in an organization's financial position between two balance sheet dates.

The basic layout for a bank statement of changes in financial position is:

Cash & Due From (or Funds) (beginning of period)
+/–   Funds Flow from P & L
  –   Funds Used for Dividends
±/–   Funds Flow Effects of Changes in Balance Sheet
  =   Funds (end of period)

Many accountants consider the statement of changes an unnecessary component of bank financial statements, since it reflects only net changes which can be easily calculated by comparing the current and prior year's balance sheet. This statement does provide useful information for purposes of analysis. It makes it easy to determine changes in key factors and their effect on the bank's operations.

A bank's statement of changes in forms the reader as to the net increase or decrease in a bank's earning assets along with the increases or decreases in individual categories of earning assets. Since a bank's income is its net interest income (difference between income on earning assets and expense on interest-bearing liabilities), a comparison of the net increase or decrease in earning assets with the increase or decrease in total assets should provide information about the relative increase or decrease in a bank's earning power.

The two basic formats for the statement of changes are the cash basis and the working-capital basis. With a cash basis statement of changes the changes in the cash balance over a period of time are summarized. A cash basis statement of changes reflects all sources and uses of cash for the period and the change in the cash balance during the period.

The following three major points about a cash basis statement of changes should be noted:

1. All sources and uses of cash must be shown since the net amount (sources minus uses) must equal the increase or decrease in cash for the period. Sources and uses of cash should never be netted except for the cash received from operations where revenues and expenses are netted. It is acceptable to lump together several small sources of cash under "other sources of cash" and several small uses of cash under "other uses of cash."

2. If all sources and uses of cash are reflected, then most of the financing and investing activities for the organization are reflected. Most financing and investing activities result in the receipt or payment of cash.

3. Those financing and investing activities that do not result in receipt or payment of cash are treated as both a source and a use of financial resources. For example, if a building is acquired in exchange for stock, both the issuance of stock and the acquisition of the building are shown on the statement of changes. No cash has been received or paid but the source and use of financial resources are reflected.

The working-capital (current assets minus current liabilities) statement of changes is the most common format. Working capital is basically the excess of near-term cash receipts (current assets) over near-term cash payments (current liabilities). This provides a buffer of expected cash flows to be used before long- term financing is required. This statement shows the sources and uses of working capital for the period and the change in working capital during the period.

The following three major points about a working-capital basis statement of changes should be noted:

1. All sources and uses of working capital must be reflected since the net amount (sources minus uses) must equal the increase or decrease in working capital for the period. Sources and uses of working capital should not be netted against each other, except for the working capital received from operations. It is acceptable to lump together several small sources of working capital under "other sources of working capital," and several small uses of working capital under "other uses of working capital."

3. Most of the important financing and investing activities of an organization will be presented if all sources and uses of working capital are presented. Most financing activities increase working capital, and most investing activities decrease working capital.

4. Since some important financing and investing activities do not affect working capital, these activities must be shown as both a source and use of financial resources.

To prepare a statement of changes requires an examination of each entry that affects the noncurrent accounts for the period to determine if the underlying transaction is a source of working capital, a use of working capital, or has no effect on working capital. Transactions having no effect on working capital must then be examined to determine whether they are significant financing and investing activities which should be summarized in the statement of changes.

Some common sources of funds are:
1. Current Operations — Represents the net amount of revenues and expenses from continuing operations for the current period.
2. Long-Term Liabilities — Long-term transactions that may involve notes. mortgages, or bonds.
3. Sale of Noncurrent Assets — The sale of a fixed asset, long-term investment, or other noncurrent asset for cash or receivables.
4. Sale of Capital Stock — Issuance of stock for cash or current receivables. If the organization is a sole proprietorship or partnership, and additional investment of current assets by the owner(s), would be a source of funds.
1. Some common uses of funds are:
1. Purchase of Noncurrent Assets The purchase of fixed assets, long-term investments, or other noncurrent assets decreases working capital.
2. Payment of Noncurrent Liabilities — Payment of long-term debt such as bonds, mortgages, or long-term notes or contributions to a debt retirement fund, bond sinking fund or other special noncurrent fund.
3. Capital Reductions — The purchase of treasury stock or stock for retirement or withdrawals of cash or other current assets by a proprietor or partners.

4. Declaration of a Dividend — Declarations of a dividend to be paid in cash or other current assets. The declaration of the dividend uses funds, since the current liability, dividends payable, is created on the date of declaration.

The following points aid in the preparation of a statement of changes in financial position:

1. The basic information necessary to prepare the statement of changes is provided by the comparative balance sheets. Analyses of specific accounts are also included. The necessary information is readily available and not difficult to assemble.
2. The amount of increase or decrease in working capital is sometimes the most significant item in the statement. Therefore, increases or decreases in the individual items comprising working capital are presented in a supporting schedule of changes in working capital or included in the body of the statement.
3. Since increases and decreases of fixed assets, investments, long-term debt, and capital stock are presented, the related accounts must be analyzed.
4. The retained earning account must be analyzed to derive data relative to resources provided and applied.
5. The statement of changes includes all changes that have passed through working capital or resulted in an increase or decrease in working capital. subject to some special exceptions.
6. Typically, arbitrary writedowns, amortization and depreciation charges, and similar "book" entrics are neither sources nor uses of resources, since they involve no financing during the period.

The preparation of a statement of changes in financial position involves three steps:

1. Determine the increase or decrease in working capital for the current period.
2. Prepare a worksheet detailing the changes in the organization's noncurrent accounts and at the same time set out the period's sources and uses of working
1. capital.

2. The worksheet can then be used to prepare the formal statement of changes in financial position.

A worksheet is a convenient approach for examining all transactions that affect noncurrent accounts. The worksheet is divided into two sections, a financial position section and a changes in working capital section.

The financial position section of the worksheet contains four columns: (I) balances at the beginning of the period (noncurrent accounts); (2) debits; (3) credits; (4) balances at the end of the period (noncurrent accounts). The entries made to the noncurrent accounts, which were analyzed to prepare the statement of changes, can be summarized in the debit and credit columns. These debits and credits are then added or subtracted to the beginning balance to yield an ending balance. This ending balance can then be compared to the ending balance per the ledger to ensure that all entries to the noncurrent accounts have been reviewed.

The changes in working capital section is presented at the bottom of the worksheet. In this section sources of working capital are accumulated as debits, and uses arc accumulated as credits.

The specific steps necessary to prepare the worksheet are as follows:
1. In the financial position section of the worksheet, set up a heading "Debits" and under this heading enter the amount of working capital reflected in the balance sheet at the beginning of the period. Also enter all noncurrent accounts that reflected debit balances at the beginning of the period. Adequate space should be provided for noncurrent accounts that may have developed during the period or for noncurrent accounts with several entries.
2. Set up a heading "Credits" and under this heading enter all noncurrent accounts that reflected credit balances at the beginning of the period. Adequate space

should be provided for noncurrent account that may have developed during the period or for noncurrent account with several entries.

3. Total the debit balances entered in step one and the credit balances entered in step two. These two totals should equal.

4. To complete the last column of the financial position section, repeat steps one through three using appropriate balances at the end of the period.

5. Analyze the changes in noncurrent accounts during the period and summarize the entries that affected the noncurrent account balances.

6. After summarization, each entry must be analyzed to determine the underlying transaction's effect on working capital. Seven possibilities exist:

   a. The credit portion of the entry used to close the revenue and expense summary account should be entered as a credit to retained earnings in the financial position section of the worksheet. The debit portion should be entered as a debit on the earnings line in the changes in working capital section of the worksheet. See entry seven of the Ricson Corporation example.

   b. If an entry involves a credit to noncurrent account and a debit to a current account, the underlying transaction is a source of working capital. The credit in this entry should be entered in the financial, position section of the worksheet, while the debit should be entered in the changes in working capital section on a line which appropriately describes the source of working capital. See entry two of the Ricson Corporation example.

   c. If an entry involves a debit to a noncurrent account and a credit to a current account, the underlying transaction is a use of working capital. The debit related to this entry should be entered in the financial position section of the worksheet, and the credit should be entered in the changes in working capital section on a line which appropriately describes the use of working capital.

   d. If an entry involves a debit to an earnings statement account and a credit to a noncurrent account, working capital is not affected. This occurs because earnings statement accounts are closed to retained earnings, and, therefore, are noncurrent. Since the debit reduces reported earnings, this amount must be added back to reported earnings to arrive at working capital provided by operations. On the worksheet the credit is entered to the noncurrent account in the financial position section, and the debit is entered in the changes in working capital section on an appropriate line under the caption "Add (deduct) items not requiting or generating working capital." See entries three and six of the Ricson Corporation example.

e. If an entry involves a credit to an earnings statement account and a debit to aixauneit account, working capital is not affected. Since the credit increases reported earnings, this amount must be deducted from reported earnings to anive at working capital provided by operations. On the worksheet the debit is entered in the financial position section, and the creditis entered in the changes in working capital section on an appropriate line under the caption "Add (deduct) items not requiring or generating working capital."

f. If an entry involves both a debit and credit to noncurrent accounts, working capital is not affected. Such an entry must be analyzed to determine whether it is a significant financing and investing activity. If it is not, both the debit and credit are entered in the financing position section. If it is, the debit and credit are entered in both the financial position section and the changes in working capital section. The debit is a source of working capital, and the credit is a use. See entry five of the Ricson Corporation example.

g. An entry may involve a combination of the type discussed at a)- 0. A gain or loss on the sale of a depreciable asset would require a deduction or addition respectively, to earnings to arrive at working capital provided by operations.

7. The increase or decrease in working capital is recorded last. See entry (a) of the Ricson Corporation example. The work sheet is then extended, and the statement of changes in financial position is prepared using the last column of the changes in working capital section.

The only difference in a cash basis and working capital basis statement of changes in financial position is that the cash basis statement summarizes the impact of an organization's financing and investing activities on the organization's cash balance instead of its working capital.

The two statements are similar in that it requires three steps to prepare them. The three steps to prepare a cash basis statement am:
1. Summarize all entries for the period.
2. Examine the underlying transactions to determine if they were a source of cash, or use of cash, or had no effect on cash.
3. Examine entries having no effect on cash to determine if they am significant financing and investing activities. These entries are shown as both sources and uses of resources.

The specific steps for preparing a cash basis statement of changes worksheet are:

Ricson Corporation
Statement of Changes in Financial Position Worksheet
For the Year Ending December 31, 1987

Financial Position Section

	Balance 12/31/86		Debits		Credits	Balance 12/31/87
Debits:						
Working capital	$0	(a)	92,400			$92,400
Vehicles	0	(5)	5,500			5,500
Total	$0					$97,900
Credits:						
Accumulated depreciation —						
vehicles	$0			(6)	1,100	$ 1,100
Note payable	0			(5)	5,500	5,500
Deferred income taxes	0			(3)	600	600
Common stock	0			(2)	42,000	42,000
Retained earnings	0			(7)	48,700	$48,700
	$0		$97,900		$97,900	$97,900

Changes In Working Capital Section

Sources of Working Capital:
  From Operation:

Earnings	(7)	48,700	$48,700
Add (deduct) items not requiring or generating working capital			
Depreciation	(6)	1,100	1,100
Deferred taxes	(3)	600	600
Working capital provided by operations			$50,400
Sale if common stock	(2)	42,000	42,000
Issuance of note payable	(5)	5,500	5,500
Total sources of working capital			$97,900

Use of working capital -
  Purchase of vehicle

Purchase of vehicle	(5)	5,500	5,500
Increase in working capital	(a)	92,400	92,400
		$97,900	$97,900

50

1. The account titles for all balance sheet accounts with debit balances are entered under the heading "Debits."
2. The balances in these accounts are entered in the appropriate column for the beginning and end of the period.
3. The account titles for all balance sheet accounts with credit balances are entered under the heading "Credits."
4. The balances in these accounts are entered in the appropriate column for the beginning and end of the period.
5. The totals of the debits and credits should equal at the beginning of the period and the end of the period.
6. After analyzing the changes in the noncurrent accounts, the related entries for the period are summarized. Six possible types of entries affect the noncurrent accounts:
   a. The closing entry is debited to Earnings in the changes in cash section and credited to Retained Earnings in the financial position section.
   b. An entry may involve a debit to cash with the other debits and credits being to noncuntnt accounts. The debits and credits to the noncurrent accounts are entered in the financial position section, and the debit to cash is a source of cash. Any debits or credits to an earnings statement account are entered in the changes in cash section under the caption "Add (deduct) items not requiring or generating cash." The debits are additions, and the credits are deductions.
   c. An entry may involve a credit to cash with the other debits and credits being to noncurrent accounts. The debits and credits to the noncurrent accounts are entered in the imancial position section, and the credit to cash is a use of cash. Any debits or credits to an earnings statement account are entered in the changes in cash section under the caption "Add (deduct) items not requiring or generating cash." The debits are additions and the credits are deductions.

d. An entry may involve debits or credits to an earnings statement account and debits and credits to other noncurrent accounts. The debits or credits to the earnings statement accounts are entered in the changes in cash section under the caption "Add (deduct) items not requiring or generating cash." Debits are added to earnings, and credits are subtracted from earnings. The debits or credits to the other noncurrent accounts are entered in the financial position section.

e. An entry may involve a debit and a credit to two separate noncurrent accounts. The transaction must be examined to determine whether it is a significant financing and investing activity. If it is, it represents both a source and use of financial resources. If it is not, both the debit and credit are entered in the financial position section.

f. An entry may involve a debit to a noncurrent account and a credit to a current account other than cash or vice versa. Once again the underlying transaction must be examined to determine whether it is a significant financing and investing activity. If it is, it represents both a source and use of cash. If it is not, both the debit and credit are entered in the financial position section.

7. Identify the current account, other than cash, which are not related to operations. The changes in these account should be analyzed and appropriate entries posted to the worksheet. (Debits and credits to the financial position section). Sources or uses of cash or required adjustments to earnings to arrive at cash provided by operations are entered in the changes in cash section.

8. The last step is to analyze the changes in the current accounts (other than cash) that are related to operations. A net change is computed, and the resulting debit or credit is entered in the financial position section. The related debit or credit is entered in the changes in cash section underthe caption "Add (deduct) items to convert earnings to cash provided by operations."

Some requirements regarding the statement of changes in financial position are:

1. When both a balance sheet and an income statement are presented, a statement of changes in financial position is required. A statement of changes should be presented for each period for which an income statement is presented.

2. Working capital or cash provided by operations for the period should be prominently disclosed on the statement of changes.

3. Working capital (cash) provided by operations should be presented first with working capital (cash) provided or used by extraordinary items presented directly below.

Summary

The statement of retained earnings and the statement of shareholders' equity reflect the transactions affecting shareholders' equity during the accounting period, including the net earnings or loss from the income statement. The statement of shareholders' equity also presents changes resulting from prior period adjustments, dividend distributions, and changes resulting firm capital transactions.

The statement of changes in financial position reflects the resources provided and used by an organization during the accounting period. Specifically, a bank's statement of changes provides information on the net increase or decrease in a bank's earning assets, an important factor in analyzing relative changes in a bank's earning power.

The statement of changes can be prepared on either a cash basis format or a working-capital basis format. The cash basis statement of changes reflects the changes in the cash balance during the period, and the working capital statement of changes reflects the changes in the working capital balance during the period.

To prepare a statement of changes, each entry to the noncurrent accounts must be analyzed. These entries are either a source or use of working capital or have no effect on working capital. Transitions with no effect on working capital become part of the statement of changes, if they are significant financing and investing activities.

Some common sources of funds are income (loss) from current operations, long- term liabilities, the sale of noncurrent assets, and the sale of capital stock. Some common uses of funds are the purchase of noncurrent assets, payment of noncurrent liabilities, capital reductions, and the declaration of a dividend.

The three basic steps involved in preparing the statement of changes are:

1. Determine the change in working capital for the current period.
2. Prepare a worksheet that analyzes the changes in the noncurrent accounts and includes all the sources and uses of working capital.
3. Use the worksheet to prepare the formal statement.

A statement of changes must be presented whenever both a balance sheet and an income statement are presented and for the same periods that the income statement is presented. The statement must prominently disclose working capital or cash provided by operations.

5

Current Assets and
Current Liabilities

As discussed earlier, current assets are those assets expected to be converted to cash, sold, or consumed within one year or within the operating cycle, whichever is longer. Current assets are properly presented in the balance sheet in the order of their liquidity. Some of the more common current assets are cash, marketable securities, accounts receivable, inventories and prepaid items.

The standard medium of exchange is cash, which provides the basis for measuring and accounting for all other items. To be presented as cash on the balance sheet, it must be available to meet current obligations. Cash includes such items as coins, currency, checks, bank drafts, checks, and money orders.

Certain cash items are not presented in the general cash section of the balance sheet:

1. Compensating balances—The SEC defines compensating balances as: "that portion of any demand deposit (or any time deposit or certificate of deposit) maintained by a corporation which constitutes support for existing borrowing arrangements of the corporation with a lending institution. Such arrangements would include both outstanding borrowings and the assurance of future credit availability."

The classification of compensating balances on the balance sheet depends on whether the compensation relates to short-term or long-term borrowings. If held for short-tenu borrowings, it should be presented separately in current assets. If held for long-tenu borrowings, it should be classified as a noncurrent asset under Investments or Other Assets.

Where compensating balance arrangements exist but do not legally restrict the use of cash, the arrangements and amounts should be disclosed in the footnotes of the financial statements.

2. Other restricted cash—Cash balances can be restricted for special purposes such as dividend payments, acquisition of fixed assets, retirement of debt, plant expansion, or deposits made in connection with contracts or bids. Since these cash balances are not immediately available for just any use, they should be presented separately in the balance sheet. Classification as current or noncurrent is dependent upon the date of availability or disbursement.

3. Exclusions from cash — Items that should not be presented as cash are postage stamps, postdated checks, travel advances, IOU's, securities, investments in federal funds, and checks deposited and returned because of insufficient funds. Certificates of deposits should be reflected in the temporary investment account, since they are not available for use until the maturity date.

Cash requires a good system of internal control, since it is so liquid and easy to conceal and transport. Segregation of duties is an important part of the system of internal control for cash. No one person should both record a transaction and have custody of the asset. Without proper segregation, it is easier for an employee to engage in lapping. Lapping is a type of fraud in which an employee misappropriates receipts from customers and covers the shortages in these customers' accounts with receipts from subsequent customers. Therefore, the shortage is never eliminated but transferred to other accounts.

Another very liquid asset is temporary investments. Marketable debt securities (government and corporate bonds) and marketable equity securities (preferred and common stock) acquired with cash and not immediately needed in operations are the most common types of temporary investments. Two criteria must be met to qualify as a temporary investment:

1. Easily converted into cash within one year or the normal operating cycle, whichever is longer.
2. Management intends to convert it into cash within one year or the normal operating cycle, whichever is longer.

Examples of temporary investments are cash in savings accounts, certificates of deposit which mature within one year or the normal operating cycle, and investments in securities that meet the two criteria.

Securities are recorded at cost at the time of purchase. Included in cost are the actual purchase price, commissions, taxes, and any other costs incidental to the purchase.

Cash dividends on stock investments are recorded as revenues on the date of declaration, Stock dividends or splits are not revenues but reduce the basis of individual shares to reflect the increased number of shares held.

The purchase price of bonds typically differs from their face value. This difference is recorded as a premium if purchase price exceeds face value and a discount if purchase price is less than face value. The premium or discount is then amortized over the life of the bond. On short-term bond investments no premium or discount is recognized. Instead the bond is recorded at purchase price, since the period the bonds will be held and the proceeds to be received from their sale are unknown.

As gain or loss is recognized when stock investments are sold. The gain or loss is the difference between the net proceeds received and the cost of the investment. When bond investments are sold, the gain or loss is the difference between the net proceeds applicable to the bonds (excludes accrued interest paid) and the cost of the bonds.

SFAS No. 12 defines equity securities as "any instrument representing ownership shares (e.g., common, preferred, and other capital stock), or the right to acquire (e.g.,

57

warrants, rights, and call options) or dispose of (e.g., put options) ownership share in an enterprise at fixed or determinable prices. The term does not encompass preferred stock that by its terms either must be redeemed by the issuing enterprise or is redeemable at the option of the investor, nor does it include treasury stock or convertible bonds." Temporary investments in these marketable equity securities are accounted for using the lower of cost or market rule according to the provisions of SFAS No. 12. A summarization of the principles of SFAS No. 12 are as follows:

1. The total cost and total market value of the portfolio of temporary investments in marketable equity securities is determined each time a balance sheet is prepared.

2. A valuation allowance is established in the first period that total cost of the portfolio exceeds total market value of the portfolio. The balance recorded in the valuation allowance is the difference between total market value and total cost, so that total cost less the valuation allowance equals total market value.

3. In later periods, the balance in this account is adjusted so that the cost of the portfolio less the valuation allowance is equal to the lower of cost or market.

4. A credit to the valuation allowance results in a debit to an unrealized loss account. A debit to the valuation allowance results in a credit to a recovery of unrealized loss account. These unrealized losses and recoveries are included when computing earnings for the period.

5. When a marketable equity security is reclassified from current to noncurrent or from noncurrent to current, the security is transferred at the lower of cost or market on the transfer date. If market exceeds cost, the transfer is made at cost; therefore, no gain or loss is recognized. If cost exceeds market, the difference is recorded as a realized loss at the date of transfer. Market value at the date of transfer is then used as the new basis for any subsequent determination of gain or loss.

Non equity marketable securities are typically carried at cost. The only time they are reduced to market value is when the decline in market value is substantial and due to conditions which are other than temporary.

Claims held against others for money, goods, or services which are collectible within one year or the normal operating cycle, whichever is longer, are short-term receivables. A note receivable is a claim in the form of a written, unconditional promise to pay. Accounts receivable are presented in the balance sheet at face value less an allowance for doubtful accounts.

Receivables are recorded on the date that title to the asset exchanged for the receivable passes. In cases involving the sale of goods to customer, the date thattitle passes is dependent upon shipping terms. With goods shipped F.O.B. destination, title passes when the customer receives the goods. Title passes on the date of shipment for goods shipped F.O.B. shipping point.

Bad debts result from the fact that some customers do not pay their full debt. The direct write-off method and the allowance method are the two common methods of accounting for bad debts. With the direct write-off method receivables are written off as they become worthless. With the allowance method an estimate of uncollectible accounts is determined, and this estimate is set up as the allowance for doubtful accounts. The estimate for the allowance method is determined using sales or receivables.

With the sales method, the estimate is based on a certain percentage of credit sales expected to become uncollectible. The company uses its past history of credit sales and actual bad debt in determining the amount of credit sales that may be uncollectible.

The allowance method using receivables is called the balance sheet method of estimating bad debts. With this method the accounts receivable are reviewed and an uncollectible amount is determined. The allowance account is then adjusted to reflect this balance.

Notes receivable are classified as current in the balance sheet when payment is expected within one year or the normal operating cycle, whichever is longer. Inventory, another current asset, is discussed in chapter 6.

Prepaid items are reflected in the balance sheet at cost.. Prepaid items are classified as current assets, because if they had not been paid in advance they would have required the use of current assets during the operating cycle. Also, prepaid items am seldom material in amount and, therefore, their placement on the balance sheet has been of little concern.

Current liabilities are obligations expected to be discharged within one year or the normal operating cycle. whichever is longer. It also includes obligations that will be discharged by reducing current assets or creating other current liabilities. Common types of current liabilities are amounts owed to suppliers for goods or services, salaries payable, taxes payable, revenues received in advance of the delivery of goods or performance of services, dividends payable and current maturities of long-term obligations. Current liabilities are recorded at their full maturity amount.

Since liabilities are measurable future outlays resulting from past transactions, they involve an element of uncertainty. Because of the differences in degrees of uncertainty related to liabilities, current liabilities can be categorized as determinable current liabilities or contingent current liabilities. A contingency is "an existing condition, situation, or set of circumstances involving uncertainty as to possible gain or loss to an enterprise that ultimately will be resolved when a future event or events occur or fail to occur." Current liabilities are definitely determinable as to amount, time of settlement, and obligee.

Accounts payable are recorded when title to goods passes or service is received before payment is made. The existence, amount, and due date of these liabilities can be easily determined.

Short-term notes may be issued for goods or services, loans, advances to officers and stockholders, or plant asset acquisitions. Short-term notes issued for cash and bearing the prevailing rate of interest are recorded at face amount. Short-term notes issued for cash with little or no interest rate are recorded at the amount of cash received.

Other types of current liabilities are:

1. **Current maturity of long-term debt** — Represents the portion of mortgages, notes, bonds, and other long-term debts that will mature and be repaid through the use of existing current assets or the creation of other current liabilities.

2. **Dividends payable** — Becomes an obligation on the date of declaration. This relates only to cash dividends, not stock dividends.

3. **Unearned revenue and returnable deposits** — Unearned revenue is payment for goods or services received prior to their delivery. The organization is liable for delivering the goods, performing the services, or refunding the advance payment if it fails to perform.

An organization may receive an advance from a customer to guarantee payment of expected future obligations or performance of a contract or service. They may also receive deposits from customers as guarantees for possible damage to property held by the customers. These advances and deposits should be reflected as current liabilities if they will be realized in revenue or refunded within one year or the normal operating cycle, whichever is longer.

4. **Accrued liabilities** — Represents unpaid obligations that arose as a result of tax legislation, past contractual commitments, or past services received.

5. **Income taxes** — Represents income taxes payable according to the tax return. Contingent liabilities are dependent upon the occurrence or nonoccurrence of one or more future events to confirm the amount payable, or the payee, or the

date payable, or its existence. With a loss contingency, the chance of the future event or events confirming the impairment of an asset or incurrence of a liability may be probable (likely to occur), reasonably possible (morn than remote but less than likely), or remote (slight chance of occurring).

A loss contingency should be accrued only if it meets both of the following conditions:
1. Prior to issuance of the financial statements available information indicates that an asset has been impaired or a liability incurred at the date of the financial statements.
2. A reasonable estimation of the loss can be obtained.
1. Loss contingencies include product warranties, coupons and trading stamps, gift certificates, service contracts, and litigation claims, and assessments.

Gains contingencies are not recorded. Gains are recorded only when realized.
Current liabilities are generally reflected on the balance sheet in order of maturity or according to amount (largest to smallest). However, bank overdrafts and short term notes payable are usually shown first, followed by trade accounts payable.

As discussed in an earlier chapter, bank assets and liabilities are not classified as current and noncurrent.

A bank's balance sheet under the caption "Cash and Due from Other Banks" should include currency and coin, cash items in process of collection, demand account balances with other banks, and time and savings account balances with other banks. Cash items that are not payable immediately in cash upon presentation with the United States, or the collection of which is contingent upon the occurrence of other events should be classified as "Other Assets" or "Loans." Restrictions on cash arising from Federal Reserve Board or state reserve requirements need not be disclosed. Other restrictions, however, should be disclosed.

Most banks cannot invest in equity securities, with the exception of some mutual savings banks and state banks. These banks must record their marketable equity securities at lower of aggregate cost or aggregate market. Marketable debt securities are typically carried at cost. The purchases and sales of investment securities can be recorded on either settlement date or trade date. Most banks use the settlement date for convenience, but the trade date is preferable. A bank is obligated to buy or sell securities as of the trade date and, therefore, the transaction should be recorded at that time.

Most banks do not provide a valuation allowance for a decline in the market value of its investment securities, since they expect to hold the securities until maturity. In times of economic uncertainty, a bank with little liquidity and a significant decline in the market value of its investment should establish a valuation allowance.

A bank's balance sheet should reflect investment securities at cost adjusted for amortization of premiums and accretion of discounts. Also, the market value of investment securities by class should be disclosed.

Trading account securities are securities purchased with the intent of reselling them within a short period of time. Regulatory authorities permit banks to carry these securities at current market value, or at lower of cost or market. The most widely used method is lower of cost or market.

A bank may have many types of loans such a commercial loans, installment loans, real estate loans, leasing transactions, and credit card transactions. These different loans require different methods of accounting.

An allowance for possible loan losses must be established. The allowance should equal the difference between a bank's recorded investment in a problem loan and the fair value of the underlying collateral. The allowance should be adequate to cover the loan balances and any potential loss of accrued interest receivable.

Other assets on a bank's balance sheet include:

1. Investments in subsidiaries — Accounted for using either the equity method or the cost method depending on the extent of the investment and the influence the investor has over the subsidiary.
2. Customers' liability on acceptances outstanding
3. Repossessions — Recorded at lower of cost or market at the time of repossessions.
4. Cash items not in process of collection.
5. Purchased interest on securities
6. Cash surrender value of life insurance—Amount recorded can be found in a schedule within the insurance policy or obtained from the insurance carrier.
7. Interest receivable
8. Trust income receivable
9. Prepaid expenses
10. Accounts receivable
11. Inventories
12. Deferred charges

Deposits on a bank's balance sheet can be reflected in the liabilities section as a one-line item or broken down by type of account or depositor. The dollar amount of certificates of deposit of $100,000 or more must be disclosed.

Repurchase agreements and federal funds purchased play a vital role in a bank's management of cash reserves. Under a repurchase agreement a bank agrees to sell securities from its portfolio to a customer but agrees to repurchase the securities at a specified date. Federal funds are typically purchased from another bank on a shon-term basis.

Other liabilities for a bank include:

1. Dividends payable — Should be recorded at date of declaration.
2. Minority interest in consolidated subsidiaries — If material, should be shown separately on the balance sheet before stockholder's equity.
3. Interest payable
4. Income taxes payable
5. Property taxes payable
6. Accounts payable

The most common types of bank indebtedness are capital notes, borrowings from the Federal Reserve Bank, long-term mortgages, commitments under capital leases, treasury tax and loan notes payable, installment and contract purchases, and commercial paper. Interest-bearing demand notes issued to the U. S. Treasury must be reflected separately on the balance sheet from other liabilities for borrowed money. The balance sheet may include a detail listing of notes payable or a summary classification.

Summary

Assets are classified as current if an organization express to convert them to cash, sell them, or consume them within one year or with the operating cycle, whichever is longer. Current assets are presented on the balance sheet in order of liquidity. The most common current assets are cash, marketable securities, accounts receivable inventories, and prepaid items.

To include an item in cash on the balance sheet, it must be available to meet current obligations. Cash items that are not included in the general cash section of the balance sheet include compensating balances and cash restricted for special purposes. Postage stamps, postdated checks, travel advances, IOU's, securities, investments in federal funds, and NSF checks are not considered cash. The liquidity of cash necessitates a strong system of internal control.

)rary investment, an asset must meet two criteria:

tible into cash within one year or the operating cycle, whichever is

2.   ent intends to convert it into cash within one year or the operating cycle.

Securities are recorded at cost at the time of purchase. Cash dividends on stock investments are recorded as revenue on the date of declaration. Short-term bond investments are recorded at their purchase price, and no premium or discount is recognized. A gain or loss on stock investments is recognized when they sold. SFAS No. 12 defines equity securities which are accounted for using the lower of cost or market rule. Non equity marketable securities are typically carried at cost.

Short-term receivables are claims held against others for money, goods, or services collectible within one year or the normal operating cycle, whichever is longer. An organization records a receivable on the date that title to the asset exchanged for the receivable passes. Accounts receivable that arc not collectible are bad debts and are accounted for by the direct write-off method or the allowance method. The allowance method uses either sales or receivables to estimate bad debts.

Prepaid items, recorded on the balance sheet at cost, are considered current because if they had not been paid in advance they would have required the use of current assets during the operating cycle.

Liabilities are classified as current if they are obligations expected to be discharged within one year or the normal operating cycle, which ever is longer. Current liabilities also include obligations that will be discharged by reducing current assets or creating other current liabilities. Common types are accounts payable, taxes payable, revenues not yet earned, dividends payable, and current maturities of long- term obligations. Current liabilities are recorded at their full maturity value. Two categories of current liabilities, determinable and contingent, are used to distinguish the different levels of uncertainty involved. Current liabilities are shown on the balance sheet in order of maturity or according to amount.

Bank accounting does not classify assets and liabilities as current or noncurrent. On a bank balance sheet the category "Cash and Due from Other Banks" should include currency and coin, cash items in process of collection, demand account balances with other banks, and time and savings account balances with other banks. The category "Other Assets" or "Loans" should include items not immediately payable in cash upon presentation with the United States, and items where collection is contingent upon the occurrence of other events.

Most banks cannot invest in equity securities. Marketable debt securities are carried at cost. Investment security transactions can be recorded on either the settlement date or trade date. Most banks do not provide a valuation allowance. A bank's balance sheet should show investment securities at cost and disclose the market value of investment securities by class.

The many different types of loans banks make must be accounted for in different ways. Banks must establish an allowance for possible loan allowances to ensure proper valuation of loans.

Other bank assets include investments in subsidiaries, customers' liability on acceptances outstanding, repossessions, cash items not in the princess of collection, purchased interest on securities, cash surrender value of life insurance, interest receivable, trust income receivable, prepaid expenses, accounts receivable, inventories, and deferred charges.

Deposits are shown on the balance sheet in the liabilities section. Repurchase agreements and federal funds purchased are liabilities that play an important role in a bank's management of cash reserves. Other bank liabilities include dividends payable, minority interest in consolidated subsidiaries, interest payable, income taxes payable, property taxes payable, accounts payable, and many types of notes payable.

6

Inventory

ARB No. 43 defines inventory as "the sum of those items of tangible personal property which are (1) held for sale in the ordinary course of business, (2) in process of production for sale, or (3) to be currently consumed in the production of goods for sale."

A manufacturing firm typically has three basic types of inventory:
1. Raw materials — The materials that undergo processing to become the end product
2. Work-in-process — Goods that are in a state of production and, as yet, not completed. It is valued by taking the cost of the raw materials involved and adding the cost of direct labor applied specifically to these materials and a ratable share of manufacturing overhead costs.
3. Finished goods — Completed units on hand for sale to customers.

Inventories are typically reflected on the balance sheet as current assets, sure they will be consumed or convened into cash within 01 year or tic normal operating cycle. Since current assets are reported in descending onier of liquidity, inventories are reported after accounts receivable.

From management's view inventories are an extremely important asset In manufacturing and retail organizations inventory is most likely the largest current asset and may be a large part of the company's total assets. A potential loss exists if unsalable inventory accumulates. If a customer orders products not available in the desired quantity, style, or quality, sales and customers may be lost. Excessive or unsalable inventories may result from an inefficient purchasing procedure, faulty manufacturing techniques, or inadequate sales efforts. Therefore, maixagenient is extremely interested in inventory planning and control.

An AICPA committee stated: "A major objective of accounting for inventories is the proper determination of income through the process of matching appropriate costs against revenues." In relationship to inventory, the matching process consists of determining how much of the cost of goods available for sale during the period should be deducted from current revenues and how much should be carried forwani as inventory to be matched against future revenues.

Cost of goods should is computed by deducting ending inventory from cost of goods available for sale. Gross margin can then be computed by subtracting cost of goods sold from sales revenue. Other expenses axe deducted from gross margin to determine net income for the period, Therefore, net income for a period depends directly upon the valuation of ending inventory. If ending inventory is overstated, assets, gross margin, net income, and owners' equity will be overstated; and cost of goods sold will be understated. If ending inventory is understated, assets, gross margin, net income, and owners' equity will be understated; and cost of goods sold will be overstated.

Example of overstatement of ending inventory:

For Year Ended December 31, 1987

	Ending Inventory Correctly Stated		Ending Inventory Overstated by $50,000	
Sales		$1,100,000		$1,100,000
Beginning inventory	$630,000		$630,000	
Purchases	520,000		520,000	
Cost of goods available for sale	$1,150,000		$1,150,000	
Ending inventory	580,000		630,000	
Cost of goods sold		570,000		520,000

The following are definitions of some of the basic concepts and terms related to inventory:

1. Perpetual inventory system — With a perpetual inventory system, the inventory balance is readily available at any point in time. Any inventory shortages can be determined by comparing inventory quantities per a physical count and the quantities as shown in the inventory records. Unless the record keeping costs are prohibitive, the perpetual inventory system is the preferred method.

2. Periodic inventory system — With a periodic inventory system, that balance on hand during the period is not maintained. A physical inventory is performed at the end of the period, and the balance in the inventory account is updated. This method is generally less time consuming than the perpetual system.

3. Purchase discounts — Discounts from the invoice price of goods given for making payment within a certain period of time. These discounts should be taken as they can translate into substantial rates of interest. An example of a purchase discount is "2/10. n/30," which means that if payment is made within ten days the customer can deduct a 2% discount or pay the entire amount ("net") within thirty days.

4. Finance charges — Late charges of interest imposed on an invoice not paid by its due date.

5. Trade discounts—A deduction from the list or catalog price of $50 and a trade discount of 10%. Therefore, the buyer actually pays $45 for the item. Typically, the buyer will record inventory subject to a trade discount at cost minus the trade discount. Purchase discounts are determined on the invoice price less the trade discount.

6. Gross price versus net price procedures — Inventory may be recorded at the invoice price (gross price) or at invoice price less the purchase discount (net price). The net price procedure is preferred for two reasons: (1) the accounts show the amount most likely to be paid. since most organizations take advantage of purchase discounts; and (2) this procedure emphasizes the discounts lost instead of discounts taken, which is consistent with the principle of management by exception.

Inventory costs include all costs incurred in bringing the goods to the buyer's place of business and converting the goods to a salable condition. Therefore, inventory costs include:

1. Seller's invoice price less purchase discount.
2. Cost of insurance on goods while in transit.
3. Transportation charges when paid by the buyer.
4. Handling costs.

In assigning a total cost to inventory, there are four cost selection methods from which to choose. These methods are based on differing systematic inventory flow assumptions. The four inventory costing methods am:

1. Specific identification — This method assigns a known actual cost to an identifiable unit of product. The costs of the specific items sold are included in the cost of goods sold, and the costs of the specific units on hand are included in inventory. This method is impractical unless the different purchases can be separated physically. It can be used in situations where an organization sells a small quantity of high-priced, easily distinguishable items.

2. Weighted-average method — This method assigns a cost to inventory items based on the average cost of all similar goods available during the period. The weighted-average unit cost is computed by adding beginning inventory to number of units purchased and dividing by the total cost of goods available for sale. The cost of total inventory is determined by multiplying this unit cost times the number of units in ending inventory

3. First-in, first-out (FIFO) — FIFO assumes that the first units purchased are the first units sold. The costs of the first goods acquired are the first costs charged to cost of goods sold when goods are actually sold. With the FIFO method, inventory contains the cost of the most recent purchases. The advantages of FIFO are (1) it is easy to apply under the periodic and perpetual systems (2) it is logical since the first units purchased are usually the first units sold (3) it cannot be manipulated like some of the other methods and (4) it usually results in an inventory balance that approximates the current replacement cost of the inventory. The major disadvantage of FIFO occurs when prices are fluctuating. With FIFO old inventory costs are being matched with current prices.

4. Last-in, first-out (LIFO) —LWO assumes that the last units purchased are the first units sold. The costs of the last goods acquired axe the first costs charged to cost of goods sold when goods are actually sold. Therefore, ending inventory consists of the older costs. The two advantages of LIFO are: (I) it attempts to match current costs with current revenues, which results in a better measure of earnings during fluctuating prices and (2) it results in lower taxable income during times of rising prices. LIFO does have some major disadvantage tages: (1) the practical application may be complex (2) earnings may be manipulated easily (3) in trying to manipulate earnings, management may make or forego purchases which could result in economic harm to the company and (4) when prices are rising the inventory balance may become. unrealistically low since inventory cost is based on the earliest purchases.

The major objective in choosing an inventory costing method is to choose the method which most clearly reflects periodic income. Some organizations may use different assumptions for each type of inventory to more deafly reflect earnings.

The internal Revenue Code requires that if LIFO is used for tax purposes, then it must be used for financial accounting.

To comply with the consistency concept, once an organization chooses a method it must continue to use that method. Before an organization can change methods, it must show that the new method is preferable. If a change is made, the nature Of the change. justification for the change, and the effect of the change on net income must be disclosed in the notes to the financial statements.

Generally, historical cost is used to value inventories and cost of goods sold. In Certain circumstances, though, departure from cost is justified. Some other methods of costing inventory are: -

1. Net realizable value — Damaged, obsolete, or shopworn goods should never be canied at an amount greater than net realizable value. Net realizable value is equal to the estimated selling price of an item minus all costs to complete and dispose of the item.

2. Lower of cost or market — If the value of inventory declines below its historical cost, then the inventory should be written down to reflect this loss. A departure from the historical cost principle is required when the future utility of the item is not as great as its original cost When the purchase price of an item falls, it is assumed that its selling price has or will fall. The loss of the future utility of the item should be charged against the revenues of the period in which it occurred. Market in this context generally means the replacement cost of the item. However, market cost is limited by a floor and ceiling cost. Market cannot exceed net realizable value, which is estimated selling price minus the cost of completion and disposal. Market can not be less than net realizable value minus a normal profit margin. Lower of cost or market can be applied to each inventory item, each inventory class, or total inventory.

3. Estimating inventory. An organization may estimate its inventory to compare with physical inventories to determine whether shortages exist, to determine the amount of inventory destroyed in a fire or stolen, or to obtain an inventory cost figure to use in monthly or quarterly financial statements. Two methods of estimating inventory am the gross margin method and the retail inventory method.

The gross margin method is based on the assumption that the relationship between gross margin and sales has been fairly stable. Gross margin rates from prior periods are used to calculate estimated gross margin; The estimated gross margin is deducted from sales to determine estimated cost of goods sold. Estimated cost of goods sold is then deducted from cost of goods available for sale to determine estimated inventory cost.

The retail inventory method is used by organizations that mark their inventory with selling prices. These prices are converted to cost using a cost4njce ratio. The cost/price ratio is simply what proportion cost is to each sales dollar. This cost/price ratio is applied to ending inventory stated at retail prices to estimate the cost of ending inventory.

A bank's inventory consists primarily of supplies and banking forms; therefore, inventories are not a material part oh bank's balance sheet.

Summary

Inventory is all items of tangible personal property held for sale in the ordinary course of business, in process of production for sale, or to be currently consumed in the production of goods for sale.

The three types of manufacturing inventory are raw materials, work in process, and finished goods. In manufacturing and retail organizations, inventory is usually the largest current asset and often constitutes a significant part of total assets. Therefore, inventory planning and control is extremely important to these organizations.

A major objective of inventory accounting is determining how much of the cost of goods available for sale during the period should be deducted from current revenues and how much should be carried forward as inventory to be matched against future revenues. Inventory accounting is also important because net income for a period depends directly upon the valuation of ending inventory.

Of the two types of inventory systems, perpetual and periodic, the perpetual system is preferred because the inventory balance is readily available at any point in time. However, the perpetual system's record keeping costs can be prohibitive.

Purchase discounts are discounts from die invoice price of goods given for making payment within a certain period of time. Invoice price is list price less any trade discounts. Finance charges are late charges or interest imposed on an invoice not paid by its due date.

Purchases can be recorded at gross price or net price. The net price procedure is preferred because the accounts show the amount most likely to be paid, and the procedure emphasizes the discounts lost instead of discounts taken.

The cost of inventory is all costs incurred in bringing the goods to the buyer's place of business and converting the goods to salable condition.

The four inventory costing methods are based on different systematic inventory flow assumptions. Specific identification assigns a known actual cost to an identifiable unit of product. The weighted-average method assigns a cost to inventory items based on the average cost of all similar goods available during the period. The FIFO method assumes the first units purchased are the first units sold. The LIFO method assumes the last units purchased are the first units sold. The major objective in choosing an inventory costing method is to clearly reflect periodic income. The consistency concept dictates that once an organization chooses a method it must continue to use that method.

Historical cost is generally used to value inventories, but in certain circumstances departure from cost can be justified. Other methods of costing inventory are net realizable value, lower of cost or market, and estimating inventory with the gross margin or retail inventory method.

7

Fixed Assets and Intangibles

Assets of a durable nature used in an organization's operations are commonly referred to as fixed assets; property, plant, and equipment or plant assets. These assets consist of such items as land, machinery, buildings, vehicles, and furniture.

The three major characteristics of fixed assets an:

1. They must be tangible, characterized by physical existence or substance.
2. They must be long-term in nature, a useful life of greater than one year. The investment in fixed assets (except land) is allocated to future periods through periodic depreciation charges.
3. They must be used in business operations, not held for resale to a customer. The normal basis for initially recording fixed assets is cost, which includes any costs to get the asset in place and ready for use. The cost of land includes any current cash outlay or cominitment for futme cash outlay plus any of the following costs that might be incurred: (1) unpaid taxes that became liabilities of the buyer at the date of sale, (2) option costs, (3) cost of grading the land, (4) real estate commissions, (5) costs, minus any salvage proceeds, to remove old buildings from the land, (6) title search and other legal fees, or (7) local assessments for sidewalks, water mains, sewers, and streets. The cost of a building should include (1) the purchase price or construction cost, (2) real estate commissions (3) unpaid taxes that became liabilities of the buyer at the date of sale, (4) insurance and tax costs during construction, (5) legal costs, (6) repair and remodeling costs, (7) architect's fees, and (8) building permits. The cost of machinery and equipment includes (1) the net invoice price, (2) sales tax, (3) transportation costs, (4) insurance costs while in transit, and (5) installation charges.

When a company elects to construct an asset, the amount capitalized should include direct labor, direct materials, and any variable overhead. Fixed overhead may be allocated to constructed assets as long as it does not cause the cost of the asset to exceed the cost that would have been incurred if purchased from an outside source.

Under certain conditions nonregulated companies are required to capitalize interest costs during construction. The two basic types of assets requiring this capitalization are assets constructed for the organization's own use and assets constructed for other son a project basis. To determine the aniount of interest to be capitalized, the organization' saverage investment in the qualifying asset for the period should be computed. This average' investment is then multiplied by the weighted-average interest rate for iod or the rate related to specific bonowings for a specific asset Capitalizitoxrthouto begin and continue as long as (1) expenditures are being made for the asset, (2) activittemecessary to get the asset ready for use are in progress, and (3) inteitst tis being incurred. Interest costs capitalized on a depreciable asset are added to the cost of that asset and depreciated.

When an organization capitalizes interest, the total interest cost incurred and the interest cost capitalized should be disclosed in the financial statements.

In some cases a buyer of a fixed asset will give a long-term note for all or pan of the purchase price. To properly record the cost of the asset, it should be accounted for using the present value of the consideration exchanged between the contracting parties at the date of the transaction. The interest rate on the note is used to calculate the present value. If there is no rate or the rate appears unreasonable, and interest rate must be imputed. The imputed interest rate should approximate the interest rate the buyer and seller would have negotiated in an anus-length transaction.

In a lump-sum purchase, several assets acquired in one transaction, total purchase price has to be allocated to the individual assets. The fair market value of the assets acquired is used to determine the allocation. The allocation is calculated by determining the ratio of the fair market value of the individual assets to the total fair market value. These ratios are then multiplied by the total purchase price to determine each individual asset's allocated cost.

Assets acquired in exchange for securities are recorded at the fair market value of the securities given up. If the fair market value of the securities given up is not determinable, then the fair market value of the asset received should be used.
Donated assets are recorded at fair market value plus any costs incurred to get the asset ready for use.

The exchange of fixed assets for fixed assets, whether a small amount of consideration is given or received, is called a nonmonetary transaction. The acquired asset is recorded at the fair value of the asset surrendered. If the fair value of the asset surrendered is not determinable, then the fair value of the asset received is used. Gain or loss is also recognized on the exchange. If the fair value of the surrendered or received asset is not determinable, then the acquired asset should be recorded at the book value of the surrendered asset. No gain or loss should be recognized on this exchange.
Additional costs; ranging from repairs to significant additions, may be incurred after the installation and use of a fixed asset. Costs incurred to achieve greater future benefits should be capitalized, and costs that maintain a given level of services should be expensed. One of the following three conditions must be present to capitalize costs:

1. The useful life of the asset must be increased.
2. The quality of the units produced must be enhanced.
3. The quantity of services produced from the asset must be increased.

The five major types of costs are:

1. **Repairs and maintenance**— Costs incurred to maintain the asset in operating condition. These costs are expensed in the period in which they occur.

2. **Additions** — An addition results in a better asset but does not extend the life of the asset. These costs should be capitalized and depreciated over the useful life of the addition. If the addition is useless without the asset to which it is attached and the useful life of the addition is longer than the life of the asset to which it is attached, then the addition should be depreciated over the useful life of the asset to which it is attached.

3. **Improvements or betterments** — When a cost increases the useful life of an asset or its productivity, it is an improvement or betterment. If the improve-

ment or betterment extends the life of the asset, the entry is debited to the accumulated depreciation account. If the improvement or betterment improves the asset but does not extend its life, the entry is debited to the asset account.

4. Rearrangements-. If these costs are expected to result in future benefits, they should be capitalized and amortized over the periods benefited. If not, they should be expensed.

5. Replacements— A replacement is a substitution of either an entire asset or part of an asset. The cost of the replaced asset or part and its related depreciation should be deleted from the books, and the new cost should be capitalized.

Fixed assets may be disposed of through sale or retirements. At the time of disposition, depreciation related to the fixed asset must be updated. The cost of the fixed asset and its related accumulated depreciation must be removed from the accounts. If the asset is sold, the consideration received must be recorded. If the asset is retired, an asset account should be recorded which describes the expected final disposition of the asset. Any gain or loss on sale or retirement must also be recorded.

Typically banks cannot own rental or other commercial property unless their intention is to use it in their banking operations within the near future. National banks must dispose of any property not used in its banking business within five years after acquisition.

Generally the dollar amount invested in bank premises and equipment is restricted by supervisory authorities. Most states require prior approval from supervisory authorities for a bank's investment in real estate to exceed a stated percent of its capital and surplus.

Any real estate not used in the conduct of a bank's business is reflected on the balance sheet as Other Real Estate Owned. As stated before, this property cannot be held for more than five years. The bank must obtain an appraisal on other real estate owned, and then record the investment at the lower of appraisal value or the bank's investment. If the investment is under $25,000 or is 5% or less of the bank's equity capital, whichever is less, no appraisal is necessary. Appraisals are required annually, and carrying value must be reduced to appraisal value if it is less than the current carrying value of the asset.

Generally, other real estate owned is recorded at cost If it is a nonmonetary exchange, the cost is recorded at the fair value of the asset surrendered or received, whichever is more easily determinable. Where fair value is not determinable, the recorded amount of the nonmonetary asset (usually a loan with a bank) is used to record the other real estate owned. Gain or loss is the difference between the fair value of the received asset and the recorded amount of the surrendered asset.

Assets acquired through foreclosure should be recorded at fair value, but not to exceed the recorded investment. If fair value is less than recorded investment, then a loss should be recognized.

The process of allocating the cost of a fixed asset tO various accounting periods is depreciation. This allocation relates to the expense recognition principle which allocates costs in a systematic and rational manner to the periods benefited. To calculate depreciation requires an asset's cost, expected salvage cost and usefullife. The cost of an asset has already been discussed. Salvage value is the amount an organization expects to receive, minus any disposal costs, when the asset is sold or retired. The useful life of an asset is the shorter of its period of usefulness to the organization or the physical life of the asset. Past experience is the best method of determining physical life. If an organization has no past experience with this type of asset, it may use the experience of similar organizations, engineering studies, or simulation results.

The primary methods of depreciation are:

1. Straight-line method — Straight-line depreciates the cost of an asset less its salvage value in equal amounts over the useful life of the asset. This method has the advantage of simplicity. If the service potential of the asset is used up in equal amounts over each period of its useful life, the straight-line results in a proper determination of earning. If service potential is not used up in equal amounts, then this method does not result in a proper determination of earnings.

2. Units-of-production method — With this method the expected depreciation rate per unit is determined by subtracting the asset's salvage value from cost and dividing by the total numberof units the asset is expected to produce. This rate is multiplied by the actual production of a period to determine depreciation for that period. If the expiration of service potential is related to production, the units-of-production method provides determination of earnings.

3. Declining-balance methods — With these methods a depreciation rate is determined, and this rate is applied to the book value of the asset. Since book value is used, the amount to which the rate is applied decreases overthe asset's life.

Double-declining-balance method is the most common type of declining- balance depreciation. First, the straight-line rate of depreciation is determined and doubled. This rate is then applied to the book value of the asset at the beginning of the period.

Another type of declining-balance depreciation is 150 percent-declining- balance. This method is computed the same as double-declining except that the declining-balance rate is 150% of the straight-line rate.

4. Sum-of-the-years'-digits method — The first step in this method is to estimate the useful life of the asset and total the digits through n, n being the useful life of the asset.

This total become the denominatorof a fraction, whose numerator is the number of periods of useful life that remain at the beginning of each period. Each period the appropriate fraction is multiplied by the asset's cost minus salvage value.

Typically intangibles lack physical existence and have a high degree of uncertainty regarding their future benefits. These assets have value because of the busijiess advantages of excluäive rights and privileges they providc. The two sources of intangible assets are:

1. Exclusive privileges granted by authority of the government or legal contract, which inclu&s patents, copyrights, trademarks, franchises, etc.

2. Superior entrepreneurial capacity or management know-how and customer loyalty which is goodwill.

Intangible assets are initially recorded at cost. Therefore, the costs of intangible assets, except for goodwill, are relatively easy to determine. These assets must be amortized over their expected useful life but not to exceed forty years. An organization must use straight-line amortization, unless it can prove that another method is more appropriate.

Those intangibles that have a separate identity apart from the enterpri seas a whole are identifiable intangible assets. The most common types am:

I. Copyrights — Copyrights protect the owner from illegal reproductions of designs, writings, music, and literary productions. Purchased copyrights are recorded at cost. Research and development costs incurred to produce a copyright internally must be expensed. The only costs that can be capitalized are the legal costs to obtain and defend the copyright. Generally, copyrights are amortized over a period of five years or less.

2. Trademarks — Trademarks are features such as designs, brand names, or symbols which allow easy recognition of a product. The costs to develop or acquire a trademark, except for research and development costs, are capitalized. Trademarks must be amortized over a period not to exceed forty years.

3. Patents — Patents are granted by the U. S. Government and allow the owner exclusive bcncfits to a product or process over a 17-year period. Purèhased patents are recorded at cost. An internally developed patent includes all costs except research and development. Legal fees incurred to successfully defend the patent should also be capitalized. A patent should be amortized over its useful life or 17 years, whichever is shorter.

4. Organization costs — Organization costs are incurred in the process of organizing a business. Legal fees, payments to officers for organization activities, and various state fees may be included in organization costs. Generally, amortization costs are amortized over five years.

5. Franchises— A franchise grants the right to provide a product or service oruse a property. Franchise fees that are paid in advance should be capitalized and amortized over the useful life of the asset.

6. Leases — A contract between the owner of property (lessor) and another party (lessee) that grants the right to use the property in exchange for payments is a lease. Any portion of the lease payments made in advance are capitalized in the leasehold account, an intangible asset account. Another intangible account, leasehold improvements, is established for any improvements to the leased property by the lessee. Leasehold improvements should be amortized over their useful life or the remaining life of the lease, whichever is shorter, while the leasehold is amortized over the life of the lease.

Some intangible assets, since they cannot be separated from the business as a whole, are not specifically identifiable. Goodwill is a prime example of this type of intangible.

Goodwill arises when an organization's value as a whole exceeds the fair market value of its net assets. This typically occurs when an organization generates more income than otherorganizations with the same assets and capital structure. Superior management, a superior reputation, or a valuable customer list are factors that may contribute to these excess earnings.

Goodwill is something that develops over time through the generation of these excess earnings. However, since no objective measure of the total value of a business is available until it is sold, goodwill is not recorded unless a business is purchased.

To calculate goodwill a portion of the total cost of the acquired organization should be allocated to the tangible and intangible assets based on their fair market values. Goodwill is the difference between the cost allocated to these assets and the total cost of the acquisition.

The amortization period for goodwill arising after October 31, 1970, should not exceed forty years. Goodwill before October 31, 1970, does not have to be amortized until the useful life of the goodwill becomes known.

Negative goodwill is created when the fair market value of the acquired net assets exceeds the cost of the acquired company. This excess is allocated proportionately to reduce noncurrent assets except for long-term investments in marketable securities. If noncurrent assets are reduced to zero, then the excess should be recorded as a deferred credit and amortized over a period not to exceed forty years.

To estimate the value of goodwill prior to the consummation of a purchase requires estimating future expected excess earnings and calculating their present value. The same result should be achieved by determining the present value of the total expected future earnings of the organization, which is the total value of the firm. The total value of the firm minus the value of the identifiable tangible and intangible net assets is estimated goodwill.

In the past, banks were not allowed to capitalize intangible assets; they were immediately expensed. Under some circumstances regulatory authorities now allow banks to record the value of intangibles relating to the purchase or core deposits (demand and savings deposits). Banks are even allowed, under certain circumstances, to record purchased goodwill.

The core deposit intangible is recorded at the present value of the expected future income from the core deposits over their remaining life. Core deposit intangibles should be amortized over their remaining useful life.

Sometimes, in a bank acquisition, the fair value of the liabilities assumed exceeds the fair value of the tangible and identifiable intangible assets. This excess of liabilities creates an unidentifiable intangible asset. These assets should be amortized on a straight-line basis over a period not to exceed the estimated remaining life of the long-term, interest-bearing assets acquired. If a significant amount of long-term, interest-bearing assets are not acquired, then the amortization period should not exceed the, estimated average remaining life of the existing acquired deposit base.

Summary

Fixed assets, also called property, plant, and equipment or plant assets, are assets of a durable nature used in an organization's operations. These assets are tangible, long-term in nature, and used in business operations. The normal basis for the initial recording of fixed assets is cost, which includes any costs to get the asset in place and ready for use.

When a company constructs its own fixed asset, the amount capitalized includes direct materials, direct labor, variable overhead, and a portion of fixed overhead.

Interest costs during construction must be capitalized when assets are constructed for the organization's own use or for others on a project basis. When a long-term note is given in exchange for a fixed asset, an organization should record the cost of the asset as the present value of the consideiationexegcd. When several assets are acquired in a lump-sum purchase, the total mirth .eg allocated to the individual assets using the ratio of fair market value of the fnelual item to fair market value of the total acquired assets. When secuiities am exchanged for a fixed asset, the asset is recorded at the fairmarket value of the securitietgivenup. Donated assets are recorded at fair market value plus any costs incurred to gëtthe asset ready for use.

In nonmonetary transactions, the asset acquired is recorded at, in order of preference, the fairvalue of the asset surrendered, the fairvalue of the asset receives or the book value of the asset surrendered.

Costs incurred after installation of a fixed asset should be capitalized if the useful life of the asset is increased, the quality of the units produced is enhanced, or the quantity of services produced by the asset is increased. The five major types of costs are repairs and maintenance, additions, improvements and betterments, rearrange ments, and replacements. -

When fixed assets are sold or retired, the related depreciation must be updated, the cost of the asset and its accumulated depreciation must be removed from the accounts, and any gain or loss must be recorded.

Banks usually cannot own rental or other commeicial preperty unless their intention is to use it in their banking operations within the near future. Real estate not used in the operation of the bank is recorded on the balance sheet as Other Real Estate Owned and is generally recorded at cost. Assets acquired thiough fbreclosure are recorded at fair value, but not to exceed the recorded investment.

Depreciation is the process of allocating the cost of a fixed asset to various accounting periods. The primary methods of depreciation am the straight-line method, the units-of-production method, the declining-balance methods, and the sum-of-the-years '-digits method.

Intangibles lack physical existence and have a high degree of uncertainty regarding their future benefits. Intangible assets are initially recorded at cost and are amortized on the straight-line basis over their useful life, not to exceed forty years. Identifiable intangible assets include coj,yrights, trademarks, patents, organization costs, franchises, and leases. Goodwill is the most common example of an intangible that is not specifically identifiable because it cannot be separated from the business as a whole.

In the past banks expensed intangible assets, since they were not allowed to capitalize intangibles. Now, under certain circumstances, banks are allowed to record goodwill and the value of intangibles relating to the purchase of core deposits.

8

Qther Liabilities and Equities

Long-term liabilities are obligations not due within one year or die nomial operating cycle, whichever is longer. These obligations will not be eliminated by using current assets or creating cuntnt liabilities.

The following is terminology associated with long-term debt:

1. Secured or unsecured — Secured debt has legal agreements that provide the creditor with liens on certain specified property. The lien allows the creditor to sell the property pledged as security on the loan to obtain money to satisfy any unpaid balance of interest and principal.

2. Bond indenture — A contract between the coiporation issuing the bonds and the bondholders is a bond indenture. The bond indenture includes items such as the amount of bonds authorized, the due date, the interest rate, any dividend or other restrictions, and any property pledged as security.

3. Trustee — Typicaily the trustee holds the bond indenture and acts as an independent third party to protect the interests of the bond issuer and the bondholder.

4. Bond — A bond is a debt instrument that contains a promse to pay a specified principal amount at a determinable future date, together with interest at specified times. Bonds are a good financing anngement when relatively large sums of money are required for long periods.

5. Registered or coupon bonds - With registered bonds, interest is paid to the registered owner. With coupon bonds, interest is paid to the individual presenting the periodic interest coupons.

6. Term or serial bonds — Term bonds occur when an entire bond issue matures on a single fixed maturity date. Serial bonds are issues that mature in installmenls over a period of time.

7. Income bonds— Income bonds am-unsecured debt where interest is paid only to the extent of an organization's current earnings. If interest is not paid due to a lack of earnings, bondholders have no claim against future earnings for the interest not paid in the current period.

8. Revenue bonds — Generally, revenue bonds are issued by local governmental units, and interest and principal can only be paid from specific revenue sources. -

9. Convertible bonds — Convertible bonds allow the bondholder the option to convert the bonds into a specified number of shares of common stock. -

10. Callable bonds — Callable bonds can be purehased from the bondholder by the issuing corporation at the issuer's option priorto maturity. If interest rates fall or an organization wishes to reduce its outstanding debt, thcn it may call a bond issue.

Nominal rate, stated rate, or coupon rate are all names for the interest rate stated on a bond. The periodic interest payments on a bond are determined by this rate. However, the price at which the bonds are sold determines the actual interest expense incurred on the bond issue. The actual rate of interest incurred is called the effective rate, the yield rate, or the market rate and is determined by the investment market.

Wlen a bond sells at par value or face amount, the effective interest rate and the stated rate are equal. When a bond sells at a discount (below par), the effective rate is greater than the stated rate. When a bond sells at a premium (above par), the stated rate is greater than the stated rate of the bond, then the bond will sell at a discount Iftheprevailing market rate of interest is less than the stated rate, then the bond will sell at a premium.

When a bond sells at a discount., a contra liability account, Discount on Bonds Payable, is debited for the amount of the discount (excess of face value over cash proceeds). This contra liability acëount is shown as a deduction from bonds payable on the balance sheet. This discount is then amortized over the life of the bonds by one of two methods:

1. Straight-line method — Under this method, the amount to be amortized each period is determined by dividing the discount by the number of periods in the life of the bonds. Therefore, an equal amount of discount is charged to expense each period.

2. Effective interest method —This method computes bond interest expense for the period by multiplying the effective interest rate (at the bond issue date) by the bond's carrying value at the beginning of the period. The difference between interest expense for the period and interest payable for the period is the discount amortized for the period.

The carrying value of the bonds issued at a discount increases as they mature. Therefore, the effective interest expense increases as the bonds mature, since it is based on the carrying value of the bonds.

When a bond seUs at a premium, a valuation account, Premium on Bonds Payable, is credited for the amount of the premium (excess of cash proceeds over face amount).

This valuation account is shown as an addition to bonds payable on the balance sheet. One of two methods can be used to amortize the premium over the life of the bonds:

1. Straight-line method — This method is calculated the same as it is for a discount. Premium amortization reduces interest expense for the period. The carrying value of the bonds decreases each penod by the amount of bond premium amortization

2. Effective interest method — The periodic bond interest expense Kor this method is computed in the same manner as for a bond discount The difference between bond interest payable in cash (stated interest rate times face amount of bonds) and effective bond interest expense (effective interest rate times carrying value of bonds) is the bond premium amortization for the period.

The carrying value of bonds issued at a premium decreases as they mature. Therefore, the effective interest expense decreases as the bonds mature.

Any costs incurred related to the issuance of bonds such as advertising costs, printing costs, and fees paid to underwriters, accountants, and attorneys should be charged to a prepaid expense account These costs should then be amortized over the life of the bond issue, because revenue results from the use of the proceeds over this period. -

The reacquisition of a debt security or instrument before its scheduled maturity (except through conversion by the holder) is eay'e*t$guishment of debt. Upon early extinguishment the bond can be formally ajreth,F&ld as a treasury bond.

The net darrying amount of debt is the amoumpaUIt aumatinity, adjusted for any unamortized discount, premium, or debt-issue costs. TI*4UIOUIit paid on early extinguishment, including the call premium and other itacquisition costs, is the reacquisition price of debt. A gain on early extinguishment occurs when net canying amount exceeds reacquisition price. A loss occurs wl*iTthe reacquisition price exceeds the net carrying amount. -A gain or loss on early extinguishment should be recognized in the period in which extinguishment occurred and reflected as a separate line item on the income statement.

When serial bonds are sold and each maturity sells at a different yield rate, each maturity should be treated as a separate bond issue. The entire bond issue's discount or premium should be debited or credited to a single account. The amount of discount or premium amortization for each period is determined by performing a separate computation for each maturity. Either amortization method, straight-line or effective interest, may be applied to the discount or premium for each maturity. The - amortization amounts for all maturities are then summarized and totaled to detennine the periodic amortization.

When a note is issued solely for cash, the present value of the note is the cash proceeds. The present value of the note minus its face amount is the amount of the discount or premium. The interest expense on such a note is the stated or coupon interest plus or minus the amortization of any discount or premium

When a note is issued in a noncash transaction and no interest rate is stated, the stated interest rateis unreasonable, orthe stated face amountof the noteis materially different from the current cash sales price for similar items or from the market value of the note at the date of the transaction; then, the note issued and the property, goods, or services received should be reconled at the fair value of the property, goods, or services. If the fairvalue of the noncash item cannotbe determined, then the market value of the note should be used. A discQunt or premium is recognized when there is a difference between the face amount of the note and its fair value. This discount or premium should be amortized over the life of the note, If neither the fair value of the noneash item northe market value of the note is determinable, then the present value of the note should be determined by discounting all future payments on the note using an imputed interest rate.

Short-term obligations that are expected to be refinanced onaiong-tenn basis may be classified as long-term liabilities on the balance sheet. Theitpirements for classification as long-term are management (I) intends to refinance the obligations on a long-term basis and (2) demonstrates the ability to -obtzin1he -refinancing.

Stockholders' equity for a corporation consists of contributed capital and retained earnings. Corporate capital may be obtained through stock issuances, through treasury stock transactions, by retaining corporatedearñings, or by borrowing. Capital provided by the owners is contributed capital md consists of the minimum legal capital plus contributed capital and consists of therininimum legal capital plus contributed capital in excess of the minimum legal capital. Capital which results from net income from past operations and which has been retained for the corporation's use is retained earnings. The board of directors may not legally declare dividends in excess of retained earnings.

Equities are the source of capital for a corporation. This equity capital is obtained through the sale of ownership interests such as common stock and prefened stoclc When only one class of stock exists it is classified as common stock. When two classes exist, they are classified as common and preferred stock. Each class of stock has its own paid-in capital in excess of par (or stated) value account.

When stock is issued at par value, the stock account is credited for the amount of the cash proceeds. When stock is issued at a premium (price is above par value), the excess of cash proceeds over the par value of the stock is credited to the Paid-in Capital in Excess of Par Value account. When stock is issued at a discount (price is below par value), the difference between cash proceeds and the par value of the stock is debited to a Discount from Par Value on Issuance of Stock account. When stock with no par or stated value is issued, the capital stock account is credited for the amount of the cash proceeds.

When stock is issued in exchange for a nonmonetary asset, the asset is typically recorded at the market price of the stock. The market price of the stock is usually a more objective measure. The market value of the nonmonetary asset is used when the market value of the stock is not readily determinable. When neither the stock nor the nonmonetary asset has a readily determinable market value, then the transaction is recorded at par or stated value.

Sometimes stock is sold on a subscription basis. The corporation does not receive actual cash but a contract that legally binds the purchaser to pay at a later date. The stock certificates are issued when full payment is received from the subscribers. Atthetime of subscription, an asset account, Subscriptions Receivable, is established tbr the amount of the cash proceeds to be received. The Capital Stock Subscribed account and the Paid-in Capital in Excess of Par Value account are credited at the same time.

Capital stock issued for services is recorded at the fair market value of the stock. If the market value of the stock is not readily determinable, then the transaction is recorded at the fair value of the services received.

Stockholders receive dividends as a return on their investment in a corporation. These dividends are a distribution of assets to the stockholders based on their proportionate share of ownership (number of shares held) in the corporation.

The dividend payable is recorded on the date of declaration, the date the board of directors decide to pay a dividend. The date of record is the date when the corporation determines the stockholders of record who will be eligible to receive the dividend. The ex-dividend date is the day following the date of record. Any stock acquired between the ex-dividend date and the date of the dividend payment does not grant the stockholder the right to that dividend. The dividends are distributed on the date of payment to the stockholders of record on the date of record.

Naturally cash dividends are recorded at the amount of cash to be distributed. Some dividends are distributed in the form of nonmonetary assets such as property or marketable securities. These nonmonetary dividends are recorded at the fair value of the nonmonetary asset distributed, and a gain or loss should be recognized on the disposition.

Sometimes a corporation will declare a dividend to bedistributedin the form of additional shares of the corporation's stock. Thee thanges result from such an issuance:

1. The amount of minimum legal capital increases.

2. The excess of the current market value of the stock over its par or stated value increases the contributed capital in excess of par ertawd ialue.

3. Retained earnings decreases by the amount equal to the number of shares issued as a dividend times the current market value per shate.

Stock dividends are recorded at the fair market value of the stock on the date of declaration. -

A liquidating dividend is a dividend which returns a stockholder's invested capital. The two main types of liquidating dividends are:

1. A dividend declaration by the board of directors when sufficient retained earnings to not exist. This type of liquidating dividend reduces paid-in capital in excess of par or stated value.

2. When a company is actually being liquidated, pro rata distributions are made to stockholders. After satisfying all creditor claims;pmportional distributions of the remaining assets are made to stockholders. -

When a corporation exchanges its existing shares of stock for a greater number of shares with a proportionately lower par or stated value, it is called a stock split A stock split reduces the minimum legal capitalization per share and increases the number of shares outstanding.

Example:

X Corporation has 500,000 shares of $10 per value capital stock authorized and issued. X Corporation declares a 2- for-i stock split on September 1, 1987. The entry to record the stock split is:

Capital stock, $10 per value 5,000,000

Capital stock. $5 per values,000,(X)O -

X Corporation now has 1,000,000 shares Of $5peE value capital stock authorized nd issçed.

Large stockdividends increase the number ofsharesvfacoq,oratü, 'soutstanding capital stock by more than 20% to 25%. Since a large stock dhãdend typically reduces the per share selling price of the stock, the dividend is capital jed at the par

or stated value of the stock. -

Stock of a corporation that has been issued to stockholders and subsequently reacquired by the corporation is treasury stock. Treastiry stocic is viewed as reducing or contracting stockholders' equity. On the baicç,shcet, treasury stock is reflected as a deduction from the total of capital stock, capital surplus, and retained earnings.

Treasury stock can be accountcd for by one of the folkiwing methods:

1. Cost method — Treasury stock is recorded at cost when acquired with this method. Treasury stock that is reissued above cost requires a credit to the Paid-

in Capital from Treasury Stock account for the excess of sale price over cost. Treasury stock that is reissued below cost required a debit to Paid-in Capital from Treasury Stock, if contributed capital exists from previous treasury stock transactions. If a paid-in capital from treasury stock account does not exist, then the paid-in capital in excess of par or stated value account is debited. If there is still a deficiency, then retained earnings is debited.

2. Par or stated value method — Treasury stock acquired under this method is debited for the par or stated value of the capital stock acquired. Paid-in capital in excess of par must be debited to cancel the amount of premium on the original issuance. Any excess of cost over par value is debited to retained earnings. Any excess of original issuance price over reacquisition cost is credited to paid-in capital in excess of par or paid-in capital hum treasury stock.

Retained earnings may be increased or decreased through earnings (ipsses), prior period adjustments, dividend distributions, and adjustments used to maintain the minimum legal capitalization of a corporation.

Ordinary and extraordinary earnings of past and current periods are the most common source of retained earnings. Another source or reduction in retained earnings is prior period adjustments. These prior period adjustments may be (1) correction of an error in prior period financial statements or (2) adjustments resulting from income tax benefits realized in the current period from the carry- forward of operating losses of purchased subsidiaries to the current year. The most

common reduction in retaincd earnings results from net losses.

The basic format for statements of retained earnings and statements of additional paid-in capital is:

Balance at the beginning of the period.

Additions.

Deductions.

Balance at the end of the period.

Regulatory authorities requirc banks to meet certain standards in regards to the amount of their equity. These standards vary from bank to bank depending on its size and nature of its assets.

Three major accounts— capital stock, surplus, and retained earnings — comprise a bank's equity section. The surplus account for a bank is unique because it has characteristics of both additional paid-in capital and retained earnings.

A bank's capital consists of primary and secondary components. The primary components consists of common stock, perpetual preferred stock, surplus, undividcd profits, ôontingency and other capital reserves, mandatory convertible instruments, and the allowance for possible loan losses. The secondary components consist of financial instruments that possess some, but not all, of the features of capital. Examples of secondary components are limited life preferred stock, debentures, and subordinated notes. The following conditions are requirements for secondary components:

1. The original weighted average maturity of the issue must be at least seven years.

2. Issues with a serial or installment payment program must make scheduled repayments atleast annually once contractual repayment of principal begins.

Also, the amount repaid in a given year must be no less than the amount repaid in the previous year. -

3. The aggregate amount of secondary capital must be 5O%.orless or primary capital.

Summary

Long-term liabilities are obligations not due within one year or the normal operating cycle, whichever is longer. These obligations do. not require the use of current assets or the citation of current liabilities.

Long-term debt may be secured orunsecured. Secured debt has legal agreements that allow the creditor to place liens on certain specified pmperty. Unsecured debt is backed only by the general credit standing of the issuer.

A bond is a debt instrument that contains a promise to pay a specified principal amount at a determinable future date, together with interest at specified times. The contract between the corporation and its bondholders is the bond indenture. The trustee is a independent third party who holds the bond indenture and protects the interests of both the bond issuer and bondholders. Bond types include registered versus coupon bonds, term versus serial bonds, income bonds, revenue bonds, convertible bonds, and callable bonds.

The actual interest rate that the periodic interest payments axe based on is called the nominal rate, stated rate, or coupon rate. The price at which the bonds axe sold determines the actual interest expense the issuer pays on ke.bond:issue. This rate is called the effective rate, the yield rate, or thernaitét rate. WI abond sells at a discount, the effective rate is greater than:theaixt 'Wxen a bond sells at a premium, the stated rate is greater than the ef calve rate.

Any bond discount is recorded in a contra liability account called "Discount on Bonds Payable" and is amortized overthelifeofthe bond bythe straight-line method or the effective interest method. On the balance sheet this contra liability account is shown as a deduction ibm bonds payable; thus, amortization of the discount causes an increase in the carrying value of the bonds.

Any bond premium is recorded in a valuation account called "Premium on Bonds Payable" and is also amortized over the life of the bond using the straight-line or effective interest method. On the balance sheet this valuation account is shdwn as an addition to bonds payable; thus, amortization of the premium caUses a decrease in the carrying value of the bonds.

Any expense related to the issuance of the bonds should be recorded in a prepaid expense account and amortized over the life of the issue.

The net carrying amount of debt is the amount payable at maturity, adjusted for any unamortized discount, premium, or debt issue costs. Gain or loss on the early extinguishment of debt should be recognized in the period in which extinguishment occurred.

When each maturity of a serial bond Issue sells at a different yield rate, the different maturities should be treated as different bond issues.

Short-term obligations that are expected to be refinanced on a long-term basis may be classified as long-term on the balance sheet. The requirements for this classification are management intends to refinance the obligations on a long-tenn basis and demonstrates the ability to obtain the refinancing.

Stockholders' equity for a corporation consists of contributed capital and retained earnings. Contributed capital is capital provided by the owners. Retained earnings is capital which results from net income from past operations which has been retained for the corporation's use.

Equity capital is obtained through the sale of ownership interests such a common stock and preferred stock. When stock is issued in exchange for a nonmonetary asset, the asset is recorded at the market price of the stock. This price is usually a morn objective measure. Capital stock issued for services is also recorded at the market value of the stock.

Stockholders receive dividends as aretum on their investment. Dividends can be distributed in the form of cash, additional shares of stock, or other nonmonetary assets. Liquidating dividends are dividends which return a stockholder's invested capital. A stock split occurs when a corporation exchanges its existing shares of stock for a greater number of shams with a proportionately lower par or stated value. Treasury stock is stock that has been issued and subsequently reacquired by the corporation. Treasury stock is accounted for by the cost method or the par or stated value method.

Transactions that affect the retained earnings account are earnings (losses), prior period adjustments, dividend distributions, and adjustments to maintain the minimum legal capitalization of a corporation.

Regulatory authorities require that a bank's equity amounts meet certain standards which vary according to the bank's size and the nature of its assets. The surplus account of a bank's equity section is unique because it has characteristics of both additional paid-in capital and retained earnings. The capital of a bank has two components, primary and secondary capital.

Financial Statement Analysis

The general-purpose information contained in the financial statements can be analyzed to evaluate organizations for credit and investment decisions. The tools used in financial statement analysis include comparative analysis, percentage analysis, ratio analysis, and examination of related data.

With comparative analysis, the financial statements for the current year are compared with those of the most recent year. By comparing summaries of financial statements for the last five to ten years, an individual can identity trends in operations, capital structure, and the composition of assets. This comparative analysis provides (1) insight into the normal or expected account balance or ratio, (2) infonnation about the direction of changes in ratios and account balances and (3) insight into the variability or fluctuation in an organization's assets or operations.

A type of percentage analysis is vertical analysis, which expresses all items on a financial statement as a percentage of some base figure, such as total assets or total sales. Comparing these relationships between competing organizations helps to isolate strengths and areas of concern.

Another type of percentage analysis is horizontal analysis, where the financial statements for two years are shown together with additional columns showing dollar differences and percentage changes. Thus, the direction, absolute amount, and relative amount of change in account balances can be calculated. Trends that are difficult to isolate through examining the financial statements of individual years or comparing with competitors can be identified.

Certain accounts or items in an organization's financial statements have logical relationships with each other. If the dollar amounts of these related accounts or items are set up in fraction form, then they are called ratios. Ratios can be broadly classified as liquidity ratios, activity ratios, profitability ratios, or coverage ratios.

Liquidity ratios measure an organization's debt-paying ability, especially in the short-term. These ratios indicate an organization's capacity to meet maturing current liabilities and its ability to generate cash to pay these liabilities. -

Some of the more common liquidity ratios are:

1. Current Ratio Current Assets

(Working Capital Ratio) — Current Liabilities

This ratio indicates an organization's ability to pay its current liabilities with its current assets and, therefore, shows.the strength of its working capital position. Both short-term and long-term creditors are interested in the current ratio, because a firm unable to meet its short-term obligations may be forced into bankruptcy. Many bond indentures require the borrower to maintain at least a certain minimum current ratio.

2. Acid-test ratio Quick assets

(Quick ratio) Current liabilities

Quick assets are cash, marketable securities, and net receivables. This ratio is particularly important to short-ternicreditors since it relates cash and immediate cash inflows to immediate cash outflows.

3. Defensive assets

Defensive-Interval ratio =

Projected daily operational expenditures

minus noncash charges

Defensive assets include cash, marketable securities, and net receivables. Pmjected daily expenditures can be calculated by dividing cost of goods sold plus selling and administrative expenses and other cash expenses by 365 days. With this ratio, the time span an organization can operate on present liquid assets can be measured. -

Activity ratios measure the liquidity of certain assets and relate information on how efficientlyassets are being utilized.

Some common activity ratios are:

1. Net credit sales

- - Accounts receivable turnover =

Average net trade receivables

The average receivables outstanding can be calculated by using the beginning and ending balance of the trade receivables. This ratio provides information on the quality of an organization's receivables and how successful it is in collecting outstanding receivables. A fast turnover lends credibility to the current ratio and acid-test ratio.

2. Cost of goods sold

inventory turnover = _____

- Average inventory

The inventory turnover indicates how quickly inventory is sold. Typically, a high turnover indicates that an organization is performing well. This ratio can be used in determining whether them is obsolete inventory or if pricing problems exist The use of different inventory valuation methods (LIFO, FIFO, etc.) can affect the turnover ratio.

3. Net Sales

Total assets turnover = -

Average total assets

The total assets turnover indicates how efficiently an organization utilizes its capital invested in assets. A high turnover ratio indicates that an organization is effectively using its assets to generate sales.

Profitability ratios are the ultimate test of management's effectiveness. They indicate how well an organization operated during a year. Typically these ratios are calculated using sales or total assets.

Common profitability ratios are:

This ratio indicates the proportion of the sales dollar that remains after deducting expenses. The use of this ratio with the asset turnover ratio calculates the rate of return on total assets.

2. Rate of return Net income. on total assets =

Net sales

Net Income to average

Net Sales Net Income

x =

Total Avg. Assets Total Avg. Assets

stockholders' equIty Average stockholders' equity

This ratio is often called return on equity (ROE) and is important to stockholders as a measure of the income-producing ability of an organization. This ratio reflects the return earned by an organization on each dollar of-owners' equity invested.

Net income minus current year preferred dividends

Earnings per share is probably the most widely used ratio for evaluating an organization's operating ability. The complexity of the calculation of Efl is determined by a corporation's capital structure. An organization with no outstanding convertible securities, warrants, or options has a simple capital structure. An organization has a complex structure if it has such items outstanding. The investor should be careful not to concentrate on this number to the exclusion of the organization as a whole. One dangerin concentrating on this number is that EPS can easily be increased by purchasing treasury stock which reduces outstanding shares.

Analysts and investors use this valu&to detennine whether a stock is overpriced or underpriced. Different analysts have differing views as to the proper P/E ratio for a certain stock or the future earnings prospects of the firm. Several factors such as relative risk, trends in earnings, stability of earnings, and the market's perception of the growth poternial of the stock affect the P/E ratio.

Cash dividends

Payout ratIo = or

Net income

Dividend per share

Depending on their tax status certain Investors are attracted to the stock of organizations that pay out a large percentage of their earnings, and others are attracted to organizations that retain and reinvest a large percentage -of their earnings., Growth organizations typicafly reinvest a large• percentage of their earnings; therefore, they have low payout ratios.

1.

Net income Profit margin on sales =

Net sales

3.

The rate of return increases the more a company earns per dollar of sales and the more sales it makes per dollar invested in operating assets. -

Net income

4.

Earnings per share =

Weighted-average number of shares outstanding

5.

PrIce-earnings ratIo =

Market price of stock

Earnings per share

6.

EPS

Coverage ratios are used in predicting the long-mn solvency of organizations. Bondholders are interested in these ratios, because they pmvide some indication of the measure of pmtection available to bondholders. For those interested in investing in an organization's common stock, these ratios indicate some of the risk since the addition of debt increases the uncertainty of the return on common stock.

Coverage ratios include:

1. Debt

Debt to total equity

Total assets or equities

This ratio impacts an organization's ability to obtain additional financing. It is important to creditors because it indicates an organization's ability to withstand losses without impairing the creditor's interest. A creditor prefers a low ratio since it means there is more "cushion" available to creditors if the organization becomes insolvent.

2. Income before interest and taxes

Times Interest earned =

Interest expense

This ratiO provides an indication of whether an organization can meet its required interest payments when they become due. This ratio also pmvides a rough measure of cash flow from operations and cash outflow as interest on debt. This infonuation is important to creditors, since a low or negative ratio suggests that an organization could default on required interest payments.

3. Common stockholders' equity

Book value per share =

Outstanding shares

This ratio is used in evaluating an organization's net worth and any changes in it from year to year. If an organization were liquidated based on the amounts reported on the balance sheet, the book value per share indicates the amount that each share of stock would receive. If the asset amounts on the balance sheet do not approxim ate fair market value, then the ratio loses much of its relevance.

4. Net income plus noncash adjustments

Cash flow per share =

Outstanding shares

This ratio is often used to determine the approximate amount of internally generated resources. It does not indicate theilow of cash through an organization. The noncash adjustments include items such as depreciation and amortization.

Because ratios are simple to compute, convenient, and precise, they are attractive and a high degree of importance is attached to them. Since these ratios are only as good as the data upon which they are based, the following limitations exist:

1. Typically. financial statements are not adjusted for price-level changes. Inflation or deflation can have a large effect on the financial data.

2. Since transactions are accounted for on a cost basis, unrealized gains and losses on different asset balances are not reflected in the financial statements.

3. Income ratios tend to lose credibility in cases where a significant number of estimated items exist. These estimated items include items such as

amortization and depreciation.

4. Attaining comparability among organizations in a given industry is an extremely difficult problem, since different organizations apply different accounting procedures. These different accounting procedures require identification of the basic differences in accounting from organization to organization and adjustment of the balances to achieve comparability.

Federal regulators calculate key financial ratios by using a bank's financial statements. These ratios can be used as an early warning system when a bank is approaching financial difficulty. Also, statistics and ratios on every U.S. bank am published annually.

The following are ratios that can be computed by examining a bank's balance

sheet:

1. Loans

Loans-to-deposits ratio —

Deposits

In computing this ratio, the amount of loans is calculated by adding the allowance for possible loan losses to net loans plus any direct lease financing. This ratio indicates the amount of deposits that have been committed to loans. This ratio should be viewed in comparison to other banks of similar size and in light of current local and national economic conditions.

2. (1) Stockholders' equity

Capital-to-assets ratio =

- Total assets

or

(2) Stockholders' equity and capital notes

Total assets

or -

(3) Stockholders' equity, capital notes,

and allowance for possible loan losses

Total assets

All three of these ratios can be used to calculate the capital-to-assets ratio. The first one is the traditional accounting method of calculating capital to assets. The second one includes capital notes, since they are typically subordinate to all but stockholders' claims. Most bank regulators use the third ratio since it considers the allowance for possible loan losses as a type of allocated equity Unifomi minimum capital requirements have been established by the Federal D posit Insuranàe Corporation (FDIC), Federal Reserve Board (FRB), and Comptroller of the Ciurrency (0CC). A bank may be required by the FDIC orOçC to increase its capital.

Ratios that can be calculated using the income statement are:

1. Interestincome

YIeld on average earning assets = _____

- Average earning assets

Average earning assets consists of the average balances of loans, securities, and other interest-bearing assets. Typically a bank will adjust its nontaxable interest income to a taxable equivalent basis. Converting nontaxable income to its taxable equivalent makes comparisons betweenbanks easier, since it partially compensates for any fluctuations caused by differences in asset mix. The relative risk related to the loan and security portfolios is indicated by calculating this yield. As the yield increases relative to the market and comparable banks, the possibility that the bank

holds higher-than-average-risk loans and securities increases. By comparing the changes in effective yields with changes in market rates of interest, and indicalipg of how responsive a bank's loans and securities portfolios are to changes in ma&bt

rates of interest is provided.

2. Interest expense

Rate paid on funds =

Average interest-bearing liabilities

This rate calculates the avenge cost of the interest-bearing funds employed by the bank. If the rate paid on funds is low compared with market conditions or comparable banks, it may indicate that a bank has a large base of demand deposits, that it can pay a lower rate for its time deposits (e.g., savings accounts) than comparable institutions, or both. A high rate in comparison with market conditions or comparable banks may indicate an unusually high dependence on more volatile

short-term borrowings or deposits.

3. Interest income minus interest expense

Net Interest margIn =

Average earning assets

Interest income minus interest expense

Net interest margin on a plus nontaxable income adjustment

taxable equivalent basis

Average earning assets

This ratio reflects the interest spread (absolute difference between average rates earned and average rates paid) plus any effects caused by non-interest-bearing liabilities, capital funds, and changes in the relationship of interest-bearing assets to interest-bearing liabilities. Net interest margin can be viewed as the gross profit on sales, if loans and investments are viewed as "sales." -

116

caved pud.

4. Net income plus securities gains (losses)

Income before securities less (plus) applicable income taxes

gains (losses) to avg. assets ratIo

Average assets

This ratio measures the rate of return on operating assets. By eliminating securities gains and losses, management's performance can be tested without the distortions caused by year-to-year fluctuations in these gains and losses. A higher- than-average ratio that remains relatively consistent or rises over time indicates that a bank has the ability to add to its capital base through increased retained earnings.

s. Net income

Net income to average assets ratio -=

- Average assets

This ratio measures management's ability to generate net income and is widely used in evaluating a bank's performance.

6. Net income

Net income to average equity ratio =

Average stockholders' eqUity

This ratio can also be used to evaluate management's ability to generate net income. A higher-than-average ratio may indicate a morn efficient operation or a base of capital relative to assets that is lower than comparable, morn highly leveraged banks. -

7. Personnel Costs -

/

Since personnel costs (salanes, wages, bonuses, eta) aijypically a bank's second largest expense, it is important to calculate ratios based on these costs.

a) - Salaries and related benefits

Deposits in millions

Comparison of this ratio with similar banks provides an indication of relative operating efficiency.

b) Deposits in millions

Number of full-time equivalent employees

This ratio also measures operating efficiency, which can be compared to similar banks. The increase in automation has caused greater operating efficiency; therefore, fewer employees are needed per million dollars of deposits.

8. Interest incoñie or Oxnse

Average rate —

- Average balance

This ratio can be used to detennine whether the increase or decrease in interest income and expense is due to changes in avenge balances, changes in average rates, or both.

An important ratio calculated by using the statement of changes is:

1. Dividends

Dividends to net income ratio =

Net income

118

This ratio shows both the portion of earnings paid out as dividends and the portion retained. In some instances prior regulatory approval is required for paying dividends over a certain percentage of net income. Dividends typically approximate 30% to 35% of income.

tr

Summary -

Financial statements provide general purpose information which users analyze to evaluate organizations. Methods of financial statement analysis are comparative analysis, percentage analysis, ratio analysis, and examination of related data. Comparative analysis involves comparing the financial statements for the current year with the statements of previous years to discover trends. Percentage analysis can be either horizontal or vertical. In horizontal analysis, dollar percentage differences between financial statement amounts for two years are analyzed. Vertical analysis expresses all statement items as a percentage of a base total like total assets or total sales.

A ratio is a means of numerically expressing the relationships between fmancial statement items. Liquidity ratios measure the short-term debt-paying ability of an organization and include the current ratio, the acid-test ratio, and the defensive-internal ratio. Activity ratios measure how efficiently assets are being utilized and include accounts receivable turnover, inventory turnover, and total assets turnover. Profitability ratios indicate how effectively an organization operated during a year. Common prefitability ratios are profit margin on sales, rate of return on total assets, net income to average stockholders' equity, earnings per share, the price-earnings ratio, and the payout ratio. Coverage ratios help analysts predict the long-run solvency, of organizations and include debt to total equity, times interest earned, book value per share, and cash flow per share.

Because ratios are simple to coMpute, convenient, and precise, analysts often must remember that ratios have limitations because they are only as good as the data upon which they are based.

Federal regulators analyze the fmancial ratios of banks to ensure that they are financially sound. Ratios computed from a bank's balance sheet include the loan- to-deposits ratio and the capital-to-assets ratio. Ratios computed from an income statement are yield on average earning assets, the rate paid on funds, the net interest margin, the income before securities gains (losses) to average assets ratio, the net income to average assets ratio, the net income to average equity ratio, personnel cost ratios, and the avenge rate. The dividends to net income ratio is calculated using a bank's statement of changes in stockholders' equity.

10

Use of Financial Statements

The two main categories of accounting are financial accounting and managerial accounting. Financial accounting information is used by individuals outside the organization, while managerial accounting information is used within the organization. Managerial accounting has looser constraints than financial accounting which is governed by generally accepted accounting principles. Financialaccounting is concerned with the historical, custodial, and stewardship aspects of accounting for external users. Managerial accounting focuses on management planning and control.

The financial accounting process results in the preparation of financial reports relative to the organization as a whole for use by individuals external to the organization. The financial statements summarize the history of an organization's economic resources and obligations in quantified money terms. They also provide information on economic activities that change these resources. and obligations.

Individuals external to the organization do not have direct aces to needed. infonnation; thus, financial statements are prepared. Tiey may ,flnd this needed information in annual corporate reports, infomiatitpubli$fliflusiness periodicals, or reports to regulatory agencies. EWn., useacan thom make decisions. pertaining to the whole organization such as il' extension of credit or investment in the organization.

Most organizations publish their financial statements in an annual report. The annual report provides statements on an organization's financial position, changes in financial position, and the rçsults of operations. In the annual report, the organization's auditor expresses an opinioti on the fairness of the financial statements and other information about the organization's activities, products, and plans.

The primary users of the financial sjatements determine what information is presented and how it is presented. The primary users may be either direct or indirect users. Direct users employ the financial accounting infonnationin making their own financial decisions. These individuals include creditors and suppliers, taxing authorities, investors and potential investors, and employees. Indirect users employ the information to serve the needs of direct users. These individuals include stockbrokers and other investment counselors, stock exchanges, trade associations, the financial press and reporting agencies, and regulatory agencies.

These primary users may use financial accounting infonnation in these ways:

1. Creditors and suppliers — Financial accounting information helps in assessing the credit worthiness of an organization. The financial statements include information on an organization's ability to meet its short- and long-term obligations and its earning potential. The creditor and supplier can then make a decision as to whether to extend credit to an organization.

2. Taxing authorities — Financial accounting information aids in the evaluation of information on tax returns. Such an evaluation may result in an audit or investigation and the assessment of additional taxes and penalties.

3. Investors and potential investors — Financial accounting information provides these individuals with information on the future benefits they will receive if they hold or acquire ownership interest in an organization. These

future benefits include dividend or interest payments by the organization and increases in value of ownership interests. Even though financial statements provide infonnation that is basically historical in nature, past earnings performance can be a good indicator of future potential. The present cash position as reported in the balance sheet and cash flows as reported in the statement of earnings and the statement of changes in financial position are

helpful in assessing an organization's ability to pay dividends in the future.

4. Employees— Financial accounting information aids employees in fonnulating wage demands, in deciding whether to seek employment with a particular firm, and in deciding whether to terminate employment.

5. Stockbrokers and other investment counselors — Financial accounting information helps these individuals in advising investors and potential investors whether to acquire, retain, or dispose of ownership interests in an organization. Financial statements can be used by financial analysts in

comparing alternative investment possibilities.

6. Stock exchanges — Financial accounting information can be used to determine whether to accept or cancel listings, to encourage disclosure of addi

• tional information, or to require changes in accounting practice.

7. Trade associations — Financial accounting information can be used in the development of industry statistics and norms which allow comparisons

among organizations in the same industry and among different industries.

8. Financial press and reporting agencies — Financial accounting information can be recast to providc the public with descriptive information which allows

comparison within an organization or among organizations. The financial information may be presented in a more uniform manner or trends and ratios
may be computed.

9. Regulatory agencies — Financial accounting information is used by the different agencies in different ways. The Securities and Exchange Commission (SEC) ensures that investors have reliable information to use in making investment decisions. Public utility commissions determine whether a public
utility is earning a fair return on its capital investment.

Managerial accounting is the pnicess whereby information relative to subsystems of the organization is accumulated and communicated to internal individuals (management). This information does not have to be reported in accordance with GAAP but instead can be tailored to meet the needs of specific users. The information included in internal Teliolts may range from very broad long-range planning to very detailed explanations of why costs varied from planned amounts. Managerial accounting information must be useful and must not cost more to gather than it is worth.

Since decisions are made at operating levels of thanagement. the information included in internal reports typically relates to a specific area of an organization (i.e..

plant, division, department, etc.). This information is generally forward-looking, so that it can be used in planning for the fuwre. Internal accounting information can be used in the four major types of internal management decisions:

I. Financial decisions — Managerial accounting information can be used to determine what amount of funds are needed and whether these funds should be obtained from owners or treditors. This information is also very helpful in the capital budgeting process.

2. Resource allocation decisions — Managerial accounting information is helpful in dctermining how the capital of an organization should be invested. An organization may decide to allocate a certain amount of resources to expansion of a plant, a certain amount of resources to machinery and equipment, and so on.

3. Production decisions — Managerial accounting information aids in determining what products to produce, by what means, and when.

4. Marketing decisions — Managerial accounting information can be used in setting selling prices and advertising budgets. It aids in determining where an organization's markets are and how they can be reached.

Managerial accounting information is also used by upper management in evaluating a manager's performance in such areas as cost control and profit margin.

Summary

Financial accounting provides information for external users lid must comply with generally accepted accounting principles. In contrast, managerial accounting provides information for internal use and can be tailored to meet the needs of its users.

The financial accounting process generates financial reports that summarize the history of an organization in quantified money terms. These reports provide information that external users would otherwise have no access to, enabling them to make decisions relative to the organization as a whole. Financial statements axe usually published as an annual report. The annual report also contains the auditor's opinion on the fairness of the financial statements.

Financial statements are tailored to meet the needs of direct and indirect primary users. These users include creditors and suppliers, taxing authorities, investors and potential investors, employees, stockbrokers and other investment counselors, stock exchanges, trade associations, fmancial press and reporting agencies, and regulatory agencies.

Managerial accounting collects information relative to the subsets of the organization for use by management The only requirements are that the information must be useful and must not cost more to gather than it is worth. Managerial accounting infonnation usually relates to a specific organizational area and can be used to plan for the future. Managers use this information to make financial, resource allocation, production, and mailceting decisions. Senionnanagement uses managerial accOunting information to evaluate the performance of managers.

11

Cost Accounting Concepts

Cost accounting is an impoitant part of both managerial and financial accounting. For managerial accounting, cost accounting involves the gathering and dissemination of information to management for decision making. These decisions range from the management of recurring operations to nonrecurring strategic decisions and the formulation of major organizational policies. Through the product-costing function, cost accounting contributes to the financial accounting process. Cost accounting helps fulfill the legal requirements of reporting to stockholders, creditors, government agencies, and other external parties.

To guide decisions, management wants to know the cost of something (i.e., a product, a machine-hour, etc.). This is called the cost objective and is any activity for which a separate measurement of costs is desired. The collection of cost data in an organized manner through an accounting system is cost accumulation.

Two types of costs that are gathered are variable and fixed costs. These costs axe defmed in terms of how a total cost changes in relation to changes in activity (volume):

I. Variable costs — A given cost changes in total indirect proportion to changes in activity. Variable costs remain uniform peru&tifvt4ume.

2. Fixed costs — A given cost remains .unclige4 in total tbr a given period despite wide fluctuations in activity. acd costs become progressively smaller on a per unit basis as .pmetases.

Variable costs are typicafly tboseqiøeScost that enter directly into the production process, such asiaboraadt flxed costs are costs that do not enterdii'ectlyinto aproduabaflcidi the ability to produce. The three categories of fixed costs at:

1. Capadty costs — Qjatg*iaal productive facilities and includes amortization and depieciMien of fixed assets.

2. Operatingflxed costs—tbstsquiretho operate the production process (i.e., taxes, supervisors' salari)

3. Programmed or disaeti4ffiary costs — Costs not directly related to the production process (i.e., management's salaries, directors' fees).

Variable costs can be associatedwIth activity, while fixed costs are associated with the passage of time. Banks have veiy few costs that may be classified as variable. Most of their costs arc fixed, since most of their employees are salaried. Other bank costs such as equipmeaPeosts, oecupancycosts and- other .opcraüng costs are largely fixed costs. Fixed costs remain fixed only inagivenperiodoftime in a given range of activity, the relevant range. The relevant range is the various levels of production in which certain factory overhead costs tend to remain constant. Therefore, fixed costs may be unchanged for a year or for a certain level of activity per week.

BIBLIOGRAPHY

The following books are recommended for further reading:

Frankston, Fred M. Mecimore, Charles D, and Comick Michael F, bank Accounting, Washington, D.C. American Institute of Banking.

The Book as designed specifically to acquaint students and bankers with the peculiarities of Bank Accounting.

It is also recommended that readers review a recent intermediate, managerial and cost accounting text books.

Made in the USA
Lexington, KY
30 January 2014